Other Mercifully Brief, Real World Guides
from Emerson & Church, Publishers

Raising Thousands (if Not Tens of Thousands) of Dollars with Email
Madeline Stanionis, 108 pp., $24.95, 1889102059

At heart, raising money with email is all about building your list, using timing to your advantage, crafting a series of coherent messages, presenting your email in a visually appealing way, and carefully observing your returns for clues to guide your future efforts. Do this as Stanionis advises and you don't have to be the American Red Cross or the Salvation Army to raise a significant amount of money.

Raising More Money with Newsletters Than You Ever Thought Possible
Tom Ahern, 123 pp., $24.95, 1889102075

Today, countless organizations are raising more money with their newsletter than with traditional mail appeals. And after reading Tom Ahern's riveting book, it's easy to understand why. Great newsletters have much more going for them. The essence of *Raising More Money with Newsletters Than You Ever Thought Possible* centers around seven fatal flaws. Eliminate them and your newsletter will become a powerful money raiser.

Attracting the Attention Your Cause Deserves
Joseph Barbato, 104 pp., $24.95, 1889102067

Think of *Attracting the Attention Your Cause Deserves* as a "Trade Secrets Revealed" book, one allowing you to accomplish three objectives for your cause: greater visibility, a broader constituency, and more money raised.

With more than a million nonprofit organizations in existence, there's a lot of noise out there. Shouting won't get you noticed – everybody's doing that. And everybody's tuning it out.

What *will* attract attention is following Joseph Barbato's field-tested advice. Take his insider wisdom to heart. It spills over every single page of this groundbreaking book.

The Mercifully Brief, Real World Guide to...

Raising $1000 Gifts by Mail

Emerson & Church
Real World Guides

First printed May 2005

10 9 8 7 6 5 4 3 2

Printed in the United States of America

This text is printed on acid-free paper.

Emerson & Church, Publishers
P.O. Box 338, Medfield, MA 02052
Tel. 508-359-0019
Fax 508-359-2703
www.emersonandchurch.com

Library of Congress Cataloging-in-Publication Data

Warwick, Mal.
  The mercifully brief, real-world guide to raising $1,000 gifts by mail / Mal Warwick.
    p. cm.
  Includes index.
  ISBN 1-889102-09-1 (pbk. : alk. paper)
 1. Direct-mail fund raising. 2. Nonprofit organizations--Finance. I. Title.
  HV41.2.W3785 2005
  658.15'224--dc22

                                                        2005001353

The Mercifully Brief,
Real World Guide to...

Raising $1000 Gifts by Mail

MAL WARWICK

Emerson & Church
PUBLISHERS

Also by Mal Warwick

Revolution in the Mailbox
Your Guide to Successful Direct Mail Fundraising
Revised Edition

Testing, Testing 1, 2, 3...
Raise More Money with Direct Mail Tests

Fundraising on the Internet
*The ePhilanthropy Foundation.Org's Guide
to Success Online*, Second Edition
with Nick Allen and Ted Hart

Ten Steps to Fundraising Success
Choosing the Right Strategy for Your Organization
with Stephen Hitchcock

How to Write Successful Fundraising Letters
Revised Edition

The Five Strategies for Fundraising Success
A Mission-Based Guide to Achieving Your Goals

A Word of Thanks

If you've never written a book, you may have the impression that doing so requires many, many lonely hours hunched over a keyboard, wracking your brain for just the right words as every challenging paragraph ekes its way slowly out of your brain, through your fingers, and onto the screen.

Actually, that's not the hard part at all. At least it isn't for me.

The hard part is figuring out what to write in the first place – and then getting it right. And that's not a lonely pursuit at all. That's where other people come in. Lots of them.

In the case of this modest little book, dozens of folks got involved. Clients who kindly permitted me to display their fundraising materials in these pages. Colleagues who shared their suggestions about which campaigns to feature, and which to forget. And the good folks at Emerson & Church Publishers. Especially the publisher himself, Jerry Cianciolo, who suggested this book in the first place and gave it its inimitable title.

The clients of my agency, Mal Warwick & Associates, who contributed to this book by permitting me to reproduce their high-dollar packages in whole or in part include TreePeople (Los Angeles, Calif.), Union of Concerned Scientists (Cambridge, Mass.), Riverkeeper (Garrison, N.Y.), and AIDS Project Los Angeles (Los Angeles, Calif.). I'm grateful to them all for their willingness to share.

Among my colleagues, I'm indebted to Alan Magree, Bill Rehm, Gwen Chapman, Mwosi Swenson, Dan Weeks, and Steve Hitchcock. Two deserve special appreciation. Steve and Gwen both painstakingly reviewed the draft and helped save me from embarrassment by persuading me to make many necessary changes. If they missed anything, blame it on me, not on them. It's my name that appears on this cover, and I'll take whatever you dish out in response to this work, including the blame.

Thanks for tuning in!

Berkeley, California   Mal Warwick

CONTENTS

Forget Everything You Know about Direct Mail Fundraising

Forget everything you know about direct mail fundraising. Toss aside those images of white #10 window envelopes, nonprofit bulk rate postage, garish teaser copy, and name-stickers.

Banish all thoughts of that "typical" one-percent response, $18 average gift, and 30% first-year renewal rate.

Clear the decks instead for high-dollar direct mail, and numbers that will blow your socks off. Get ready for a three, four-, or five-percent response – with average gifts measured in the hundreds of dollars and renewal rates to die for!

For example, consider the following numbers, gleaned from a statistical report on the results of an actual mailing my firm recently produced for a nationwide environmental organization:

• We mailed high-dollar letters to a total of 2,352 donors at a cost of $4.96 per piece. (No, that's not a typo. But don't freak out yet.)

• The mailing went primarily to previous donors to the organization. All but 186 had given individual gifts of $100 or more. (The small balance were donors identified in an electronic screening exercise as potential major givers.) Those previous $100+ donors fell into the following groups, defined by their highest previous contributions:

$1,000+ .... 280 donors
$500 – 999 267
$250 – 499 624
$100 – 249 995

• As you can see, nearly half the target audience (995 donors) had never given gifts as large as $250 (and most of them had never given more than $100 *at any one time*). Yet the mailing garnered 47 gifts in the range of $1,000 to $2,499, two gifts between $2,500 and $4,999, and five gifts of $5,000 or more.

• The effort yielded a total of 319 gifts, for a response rate of 13.5%. Mailings to comparable segments of the donor file using more traditional direct mail packages typically produced a response of six to eight percent.

• More importantly, the average gift in this project was $463! Revenue per donor mailed was nearly $63. Contrast that with a cost per piece mailed of $4.96 and you end up with a fundraising cost of about eight cents per dollar raised!

• It's true that 280 of the $1,000+ donors accounted for just about half of all the revenue ($73,000 out of $148,000). But it's equally notable that, of the 177 donors who had previously given only a single gift, 6.7% responded to the appeal. In other words, this mailing was effective in coaxing contributions not just from generous, dyed-in-the-wool donors but also from a marginal group of new or infrequent contributors as well.

So, "Big deal!" you, say. "You got out-of-the-ballpark returns from a single mailing to a highly selective list of donors. Isn't this just a fluke?" Fortunately not.

The mailing I've just described is, admittedly, an unusually strong example. But it's by no means an isolated one. My agency has been producing high-dollar appeals for clients since 1979.

We've mailed similar packages hundreds of times for at least 100 nonprofit organizations, charitable institutions, and political committees. And I can't recall a single instance where the response didn't justify the effort and expense.

You want more examples? Here goes:

• A 10,474-piece high-dollar mailing for an anti-hunger organization yielded 679 gifts totaling $117,749. Overall response was 6.4%, the average gift $173. The response rate and average contribution were both lowered by the inclusion of 4,449 donors who had previously never given gifts of even $100 at a time.

Both the response rate and the average contribution were markedly higher for the 6,025 donors who had previously contributed gifts of at least $100. The mailing cost $18,180, yielding a fundraising cost of only 15 cents per dollar raised.

• An appeal consisting of just 889 letters for a regional activist organization produced 28 gifts, or 3.1%, for a total of $59,450. Gifts averaged $2,123.

However, the majority of those mailed – all of whom had contributed gifts of at least $250 – had been obtained through special events, not direct mail, and were thus far less likely to respond to a mailing.

But the mailing yielded 21 gifts of $1,000 or more, including six of $5,000 or more. Fundraising cost was 14 cents per dollar raised.

• Two additional high-dollar appeals for that environmental organization I cited at the outset produced response rates of 13.3% and 12.7% with average gifts of $365 and $395. The fundraising cost was nine cents on the dollar in one case, 10 cents in the other.

Illus: 1.1 - Response Device: Union of Concerned Scientists • Actual size: 7" x 10"

Union of Concerned Scientists
Citizens and Scientists for Environmental Solutions

Two Brattle Square   Cambridge, MA 02238-9105
www.ucsusa.org   ucs@ucsusa.org   (800) 666-8276

Henry Kendall Society

MEMBERSHIP ACCEPTANCE MEMORANDUM

TO: Kevin Knobloch
        President
        Henry Kendall Society
        Union of Concerned Scientists

FROM: Ms. Jane Donor
        1234 N. Main Street
        Anytown, AS 12345

                                        12345   0000

Kevin, I agree with you that addressing the threats of global warming and nuclear terrorism is of critical importance. Please accept my 2003 renewal in the Henry Kendall Society to help UCS meet these and other important challenges.

[ ] $1,500   [ ] $1,000   [ ] $ _____

[ ] My check is enclosed.

[ ] Please charge my: [ ] Visa   [ ] MasterCard

Card # _____ Expiration date _____

Signature _____

[ ] Please list my name in your Annual Report as:

_____

[ ] I wish to remain anonymous.

Please return this form with your check in the enclosed pre-stamped envelope, or mail to Kevin Knobloch, President, Union of Concerned Scientists, Two Brattle Square, Cambridge, MA 02238. Thank you for your continuing leadership support.

RECYCLED & RECYCLABLE / SOY INK   41822AB

Illus: 1.2 - Response Device: TreePeople • Actual size: 6-1/2 " x 10"

REPLY MEMORANDUM

2004—Grove Membership Renewal

To: Andy Lipkis
Founder and President, TreePeople

From: Ms. Jane Doe
123 Any Street
Any Town, AS 00000

[ ] I accept your invitation to renew my membership in the **Sequoia Circle of the Grove**. I want to deepen my commitment to TreePeople with an annual membership gift of **$15,000**.

_____

Please inscribe my name/our names as printed above.

[ ] I'm increasing my TreePeople support with a membership gift of **$12,500**.

[ ] I'm making an annual membership gift of:

[ ] $10,000   [ ] $_____

[ ] Please charge my credit card—*see reverse.*

[ ] I prefer that my support remain anonymous.

Contributions to TreePeople are tax-deductible.

04RODOE-A
0

TREEPEOPLE
12601 Mulholland Drive Beverly Hills CA 90210

100% POST-CONSUMER WASTE. PROCESSED CHLORINE-FREE / SOY INK   TPI 4-RN2

■ So, why isn't everybody doing this stuff?

Okay, now I can hear you saying "If this stuff works so well, why isn't everybody doing it? After all, every direct mail practitioner on the planet eventually learns that people everywhere love name-stickers, and now you have a hard time finding any corner of the world where nonprofits aren't mailing packages of name-stickers. Why isn't every organization sending out these 'high-dollar mailings' you're talking about?"

Good point! But the answer is clear and almost too obvious:

• In the nonprofit sector there is an obsession about fundraising's *cost* – as opposed to its *cost-effectiveness*.

Time and again, my colleagues and I come up against development directors, chief executives, or trustees who simply will not spend what it takes to succeed in high-dollar direct mail. "Five dollars per package? You've got to be kidding! Our board will never approve that."

• Even when decision-makers have escaped the cost-obsessiveness bug, there's that little matter of the budget that so often intrudes on well-considered plans.

Faced with a choice between spending, say, $25,000 on a high-dollar mailing to 5,000 donors or, instead, spending it on mailing an additional 75,000 donor-acquisition letters, many direct marketing managers – or their consultants – will display a bias for broad reach over high touch.

• Most large nonprofits build silos around their fundraising, marketing, communications, and other, related activities. Too often, fundraising itself is split among several offices – membership or direct marketing in one, major gifts in another, planned giving in a third, and so forth.

In these circumstances, the people I call "high-dollar donors" tend to straddle departments, and a high-dollar direct mail fundraising program of the sort I'm writing about in this book may become impossible to manage.

The truth is, in all too many nonprofits, donors are arbitrarily split between those whose highest lifetime gift (or cumulative annual giving) is less than, say, $1,000, and those whose giving is at that level or higher.

One group, the bulk of the file, stays in the membership or direct marketing program. The other is shunted off to the major gifts department where, far too often, they are largely forgotten (or at least not contacted with the frequency they deserve).

In any case, most major donor fundraisers have a strong bias against communicating by mail. In such circumstances, high-dollar direct mail—which is, after all, tainted by being a form of direct marketing – is highly unlikely to be considered for the very donors who will best respond to it.

• Crass motives enter the scene, too. The fact is, most direct mail consulting agencies make their money on volume: the bigger the mailings, the more profit. A high-dollar mailing of 3,000 or 5,000 letters holds no charm for most consultants, for whom a labor-intensive project of this sort would be a sure money-loser. Most direct mail fundraising practitioners operate as marketers, not fundraisers. Volume drives the train. Donor stewardship rides in the caboose.

And there's the rub, from a fundraising perspective. Everything we learn about donors from surveys, focus groups, interviews, feasibility studies, academic research, and cocktail party conversation makes it absolutely clear that direct mail fundraising as it is routinely practiced by the overwhelming majority of nonprofits on the planet leaves much to be desired *from the donor's point of view*.

Unsolicited donor complaint mail and phone calls confirm that finding, sometimes in genuinely pungent and memorable language.

Solicitations seem to issue forth from a cookie-cutter. Low-budget "freemiums" abound. Messages offer easy, instant "solutions" entirely beyond the realm of credibility. ("Your $15 gift will save this child's life!") Gift acknowledgements are typically mailed weeks late, if at all. Even "personalization" rarely bears any resemblance to anything personal.

That stuff still works, of course – otherwise, we wouldn't be likely to keep doing it. But many direct mail donors respond purely out of loyalty or habit. And it's working increasingly less well – and hardly at all with the most sophisticated donors ... the ones with the deepest pockets.

Now, we might avoid all the work involved in high-dollar mail and other efforts calculated to cultivate our biggest potential donors if we merely wanted to secure the largest possible gifts from a limited number of donors in the shortest possible period of time.

But the true value of these activities lies in building *long-term relationships* with those donors. A gift of $1,000 or $10,000 from a high-dollar donor today may be a big deal for your organization.

But those sums pale in comparison with the thousands, tens of thousands or even hundreds of thousands of dollars you might receive from him in the years ahead if you succeed in persuading him that his big initial gift was just an initial investment – a down payment, if you will – on a lifetime relationship that may culminate with the major bequest. That's where the real money lies in any fundraising program. (I'll discuss this subject in detail in Chapter 3.)

Enough of all this theory and speculation! Unquestionably, what you want to know is, will this technique work for your organization?

■ Will high-dollar direct mail work for you?

Well, maybe not. High-dollar direct mail is no silver bullet. You can't simply point it at your fundraising challenges and expect them to flee.

But before you curse my name and rush to get a refund on this book, please give me a chance to explain.

For starters, you need a base to build on – a pool of prospective major donors who can be approached through a high-dollar program and coaxed to move up the giving ladder. Except in the rarest of circumstances, high-dollar direct mail is unlikely to work in the absence of an ongoing membership or small-donor fundraising program.

From time to time, my colleagues and I have managed to build high-dollar direct mail programs from scratch, but the circumstances were truly exceptional in all those cases.

Are you wondering about those rare exceptions, perhaps hoping against hope that your organization will fit among them? It might, but only if you are raising funds for a dramatic new initiative (or a brand new nonprofit) with blue-ribbon support – and, most importantly, access to lists of $100+ or $250+ donors from like-minded nonprofits that want to help you get your project off the ground.

Without the right sort of list access, you're unlikely to succeed no matter how spectacular your initiative and inspiring your organization's leadership.

Equally important, you'll make a big mistake if you look to high-dollar direct mail as a way to rescue a moribund fundraising program. If your organization or institution doesn't have what it takes to recruit and retain donors or members, it would be surprising if high-dollar direct mail would work for you.

You need to have a compelling case for giving, credible leadership, name recognition, and an evocative vision (and, if possible, an enviable track record as well). Otherwise, high-dollar direct mail probably won't work any better than any other fundraising technique you choose to employ.

And then there's the issue of numbers. If your organization has just a few hundred or even a few thousand members or low-dollar donors, and if you can't secure a significant number of additional prospects to flesh out the effort, you may not have a large enough pool of prospective high-dollar donors to justify the production costs of a typical high-dollar direct mail program.

But that doesn't mean you'll be left out in the cold! *With careful attention to detail and a willingness to use a lot of elbow grease, you may still be able to make effective use of high-dollar direct mail by doing much of the work by hand.*

If none of these factors poses a barrier for you, then chances are excellent you can make high-dollar direct mail work for you. Read on to find out how.

In the following chapter, I'll show you, page by page, a classic high-dollar direct mail fundraising package to set the tone for the discussion. Then, in Chapter 3, "Putting high-dollar mail in its proper place," I'll help you envision the unique and critical role that high-dollar direct mail fundraising can play in the larger context of your overall development program.

Following that, in Chapter 4, "This is not your grandfather's direct mail," I'll lay out as straightforwardly as I can the ways in which high-dollar direct mail is different from traditional, small-donor direct mail.

Afterward, in Chapter 5, I'll take you on "A guided tour through a high-dollar appeal," reproducing and describing, element by element, what went into one successful high-dollar package, and why.

In Chapter 6, "Bringing your high-dollar program to life," I'll discuss the strategic issues involved in a high-dollar direct mail fundraising program – the steps you need to take to ensure that your high-dollar mailings build on one another and help you get the most from your fundraising efforts.

The following chapter, "Sustaining your returns over the long haul," deals with the four essential elements of a successful long-term high-dollar direct mail fundraising program.

Finally, in Chapter 8, "So, why does this stuff work?", I'll take a crack at explaining – guessing, really – why high-dollar direct mail does so much better a job of upgrading donors than more traditional efforts.

Enjoy! I hope this book helps you raise lots more money. (After all, why else would I write it?)

A Bird's-Eye View of a Classic High-Dollar Package

In the course of nearly a quarter-century of writing and producing high-dollar direct mail fundraising packages, my colleagues and I have had the privilege to work with hundreds of nonprofit organizations as well as dozens of political candidates and committees.

The overwhelming majority have asked us to help them build high-dollar programs, and they've all benefited from them. Some of these programs have played significant roles in enabling important initiatives or even figuring in events that will endure in history.

But I can't think of a single time when we felt closer to the central currents of history as when my associate Bill Rehm produced the package illustrated in this chapter for The Fund for a Free South Africa.

Over the years, we've written packages for a number of well-known and important people. But none – including the half-dozen U.S. Presidential candidates we've worked for – has had the stature of Nelson Mandela.

So it's a privilege all over again to include this appeal here. It's a fitting example, too, because, at its best, high-dollar direct mail fundraising conveys the transcendent importance of the cause championed by its signer.

Regrettably, the black-and-white of these pages can't convey the brilliant colors of the original or their true dimensions. The complete contents of the package consisted of the following elements:

• A 9-1/2" x 9-1/2" blank (unprinted) square envelope constructed of bright green paper;

• A bright yellow pressure-sensitive label measuring 5" x 4", printed in black only with impact-printed "typed" name, address, and return address;

• Live, first-class postage stamps sufficient for a two-ounce package;

• A five-page letter, laser-printed on one side only, on high-quality, buff-colored stock measuring 8-1/2" x 9", with the letterhead printed in brown on page 1 and the signature in dark blue on page 5;

• A one-panel insert printed two sides in black and red on white coated stock;

• A response device measuring 8" x 13", folded in half to form a "Memorandum of Acceptance" on the top and a "Certificate of Membership" on the bottom, printed in yellow, green, and black and impact-personalized;

• A paper clip holding together the letter and other contents; and

• A #9 reply envelope, printed and addressed in black, bearing a first-class stamp.

Chances are, you won't be writing an appeal to be signed by Nelson Mandela. Your signer may not even be all that well known in your own community, let alone all across the globe. But you can still learn a lot from the structure, tone, and style of this masterful letter.

Illus: 2.1 - Fund for a Free South Africa • Actual size: 9-1/2" x 9-1/2"

Illus: 2.2 - Fund for a Free South Africa • Actual size: 8-1/2" x 9"

NELSON MANDELA
SOWETO

September 28, 1990

Mr. John Doe
123 Any Street
Any Town, AS 00000

Dear Mr. Doe,

As I walked away from Victor Verster Prison on the 11th of February, I left behind 28 years of political non-existence. Taking those first slow and careful steps, my heart was warmed by the celebratory cheers of people the world over.

I know that you were with me, and that you shared the glorious joy of my family and our people upon the occasion of my release.

During my visit to your beautiful country, I was over-whelmed with the messages of support I received from every corner of the United States. And I am grateful to the Fund for a Free South Africa (FreeSA) for giving me this opportunity to speak directly to you today.

I am writing to invite you to join me as a Founding Associate of the FreeSA Leadership Council as a way to give concrete expression to the heartfelt support I know you feel for our movement.

FreeSA is an organization that has dedicated itself to the cause of justice and human rights in South Africa. Begun in 1986 by a group of South African exiles living in the United States, FreeSA has provided a crucial link between the people in South Africa and the American public.

Through its grantmaking, FreeSA has helped sustain the grassroots projects that have fought so successfully against

Illus: 2.3 - Fund for a Free South Africa

Page two

apartheid. FreeSA will now play a key role as we begin
the process of constructing a new South Africa -- and, as a
Founding Associate of the FreeSA Leadership Council, you can
be here with us.

Quite literally, we are at the beginning of a new era in
our country. But like a ship passing through rough waters, we
are not guaranteed a safe harbor.

Our greatest strength is the unwavering commitment of the
people of South Africa to successfully navigate this course
and finally secure a democratic, non-racial country in whose
governance all can participate.

However, notwithstanding the victories which we have
recently scored, apartheid has not yet been defeated. Our
people still suffer widespread economic oppression.

Whites, who constitute 16% of our population, still
receive more than 60% of all the income. Whites in South
Africa are among the richest people in the world, while blacks
are among the poorest.

Apartheid, in an effort to reserve South Africa for whites
only, has divided up our country so that the Africans who make
up 73% of the population can enjoy property rights on only 13%
of the land.

This system has destroyed the social fabric of our
communities and left a legacy of homelessness, poverty, and
families torn apart.

Millions of our people live in squatter camps outside our
larger cities. They cannot survive in the rural areas. Their
homes are nothing more than tents or tin shacks; their children
are condemned to illiteracy, malnutrition, and disease.

Education under apartheid has meant that a generation
of children, our most precious resource, has been denied a
meaningful future. Under apartheid, white children receive
five times the resources that are allocated for black children.

The education that is offered to black children is
consciously designed to prepare them for nothing more than

Illus: 2.4 - Fund for a Free South Africa

Page three

subordinate roles in society.

   With these obstacles still in place, it will be a most difficult road to freedom. We need your help -- help that can reach us through our good friends in FreeSA.

   The negotiations which the African National Congress (ANC) has begun with the De Klerk government hold much promise. We are now so very close to achieving the freedom for which we have struggled over these many long years.

   On the heels of our "unbanning," we have sought to establish offices across our country. And we are now in a position to render visible the political influence which we have previously exercised underground.

   The millions of South Africans who have supported the African National Congress can now openly work with us to forge a new Constitution for our country -- one that will bring into being a government that is democratic, representative, non-racial and non-sexist.

   At the same time, we must begin addressing the terrible social problems that are the legacy of apartheid. I would like to tell you about just a few projects that are now emerging.

   Here are some of the programs that your contribution will help support:

   ** In the Eastern Cape, an Institute has been established that will provide advanced math training for teachers. Bantu education has denied black children significant instruction in mathematics. We cannot begin to partici- pate in the technological revolution without these skills.

   ** The housing shortage in South Africa has reached crisis proportions. Entire families are forced to live in one room. Squatter camps are everywhere. Shacks built from odds and ends gathered in waste dumps -- these are the homes of millions of our people. We are working with brick-making cooperatives to provide affordable supplies for housing construction.

Illus: 2.5 - Fund for a Free South Africa

Page four

** The children of the squatter camps in the Western Cape
have, for the most part, been denied an education.
Compulsory education does not exist for black children.
Those families who can scrape together enough money must
be satisfied with classrooms that hold 100 children and
one teacher. There are no blackboards and <u>children</u> <u>often</u>
<u>do</u> <u>not</u> <u>have</u> <u>the</u> <u>basic</u> <u>supplies</u> <u>necessary</u> <u>for</u> <u>learning</u> --
paper, pencils, books. The National Education Crisis
Committee is working with these squatter schools to give
them the help they need.

** We're planning to <u>build</u> <u>a</u> <u>textile</u> <u>printing</u> <u>factory</u> in
one of the rural areas. This factory will provide local
residents an opportunity to earn enough money to maintain
themselves and their families -- and reduce the need to
migrate to the cities in order to find work.

** Our <u>health</u> <u>clinics</u> <u>are</u> <u>training</u> "<u>barefoot</u> <u>doctors</u>" <u>to</u>
<u>treat</u> <u>the</u> <u>victims</u> <u>of</u> <u>police</u> <u>abuse</u>. In the near future
we hope to be able to turn their efforts to educating
the general public about crucial health issues -- AIDS,
nutrition, disease prevention.

The future holds much hope. But our success will depend
on our ability to muster significant economic support from
FreeSA and our other friends around the world.

We have arrived at this point because of the relentless
struggle of our own people, combined with the support of the
international community.

Today, more than ever, we need your help. I must ask you
to consider making an extraordinary commitment to me and my
countrymen in South Africa.

Will you join me as a Founding Associate of the FreeSA
Leadership Council by making a tax-deductible gift of $1,000
or more to the Fund for a Free South Africa?

I am inviting you and a small number of other leading
American citizens to join this distinguished Council because
I believe you hold the same vision shared by me, the African
National Congress, and the popular democratic opposition

Illus: 2.6 - Fund for a Free South Africa

```
Page five

movement that I represent in South Africa.

     The best way for you to give expression to our vision
is to support the organization in the United States that is
underwriting so many of our important projects -- the Fund for
a Free South Africa.

     Your contribution of any amount will give our movement the
help we so urgently need.

     It will allow us to train our young people to take their
places in the new society.  It will help us build strong grass-
roots organizations so as to assure democratic participation in
our political restructuring.

     In sum, your support is essential to our effort to develop
the strength needed to put into place a non-racial and truly
democratic society.

     We depend on the Fund for a Free South Africa for the kind
of support our movement needs.  As a Founding Associate of the
FreeSA Leadership Council, you will be helping to empower the
people of South Africa.

     With heartfelt appreciation for your support, I am

                         Sincerely,


                         NRMlandela.

                         Nelson Mandela
                         Deputy President
                         African National Congress


  P.S. Words cannot adequately express my deep gratitude, and
       that of my family and my fellow South Africans for all
       your support.  But as a small gesture of my appreciation
       for becoming a Founding Associate of the FreeSA Leadership
       Council, I'll be happy to send you a personally autographed
       copy of my book, The Struggle is My Life.
```

Illus: 2.7 - Fund for a Free South Africa • Actual size: 8" x 13"

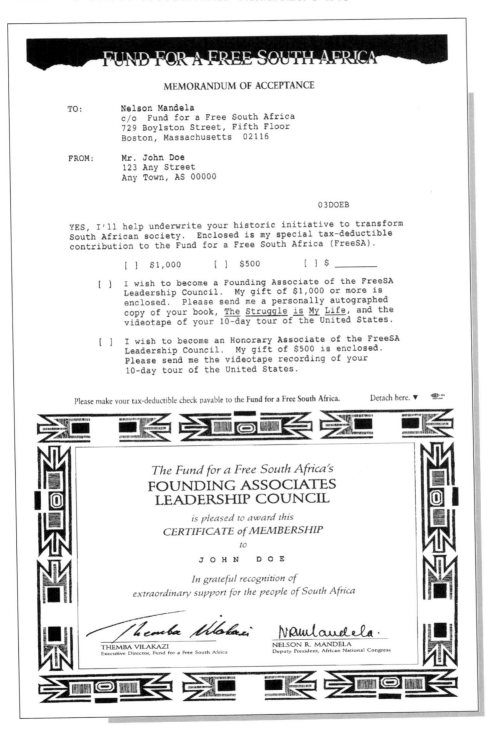

FUND FOR A FREE SOUTH AFRICA

MEMORANDUM OF ACCEPTANCE

TO: Nelson Mandela
              c/o Fund for a Free South Africa
              729 Boylston Street, Fifth Floor
              Boston, Massachusetts 02116

FROM: Mr. John Doe
              123 Any Street
              Any Town, AS 00000

                                             03DOEB

YES, I'll help underwrite your historic initiative to transform
South African society. Enclosed is my special tax-deductible
contribution to the Fund for a Free South Africa (FreeSA).

      [ ] $1,000   [ ] $500   [ ] $ _____

    [ ]   I wish to become a Founding Associate of the FreeSA
         Leadership Council. My gift of $1,000 or more is
         enclosed. Please send me a personally autographed
         copy of your book, The Struggle is My Life, and the
         videotape of your 10-day tour of the United States.

    [ ]   I wish to become an Honorary Associate of the FreeSA
         Leadership Council. My gift of $500 is enclosed.
         Please send me the videotape recording of your
         10-day tour of the United States.

Please make your tax-deductible check payable to the Fund for a Free South Africa.   Detach here. ▼

The Fund for a Free South Africa's
**FOUNDING ASSOCIATES
LEADERSHIP COUNCIL**
is pleased to award this
CERTIFICATE of MEMBERSHIP
to
J O H N   D O E
In grateful recognition of
extraordinary support for the people of South Africa

THEMBA VILAKAZI
Executive Director, Fund for a Free South Africa

NELSON R. MANDELA
Deputy President, African National Congress

Illus: 2.8 - Fund for a Free South Africa • Actual size: 3-1/2" x 8" (each panel)

Front panel

> *To relax our efforts now would be a mistake which generations to come will not be able to forgive. The sight of Freedom looming on the horizon should encourage us to redouble our efforts.*

NELSON MANDELA
Cape Town, South Africa
February 11, 1990

Back panel

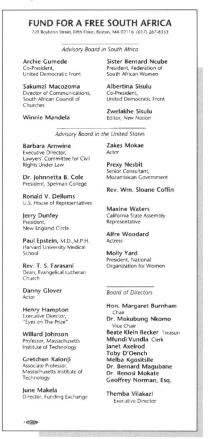

FUND FOR A FREE SOUTH AFRICA
729 Boylston Street, Fifth Floor, Boston, MA 02116 (617) 267-8333

Advisory Board in South Africa

Archie Gumede
Co-President,
United Democratic Front

Sakumzi Macozoma
Director of Communications,
South African Council of
Churches

Winnie Mandela

Sister Bernard Ncube
President, Federation of
South African Women

Albertina Sisulu
Co-President,
United Democratic Front

Zwelakhe Sisulu
Editor, *New Nation*

Advisory Board in the United States

Barbara Arnwine
Executive Director,
Lawyers' Committee for Civil
Rights Under Law

Dr. Johnnetta B. Cole
President, Spelman College

Ronald V. Dellums
U.S. House of Representatives

Jerry Dunfey
President,
New England Circle

Paul Epstein, M.D., M.P.H.
Harvard University Medical
School

Rev. T. S. Farasani
Dean, Evangelical Lutheran
Church

Danny Glover
Actor

Henry Hampton
Executive Director,
"Eyes on The Prize"

Willard Johnson
Professor, Massachusetts
Institute of Technology

Gretchen Kalonji
Associate Professor,
Massachusetts Institute of
Technology

June Makela
Director, Funding Exchange

Zakes Mokae
Actor

Prexy Nesbit
Senior Consultant,
Mozambican Government

Rev. Wm. Sloane Coffin

Maxine Waters
California State Assembly
Representative

Alfre Woodard
Actress

Molly Yard
President, National
Organization for Women

Board of Directors

Hon. Margaret Burnham
Chair
Dr. Mokubung Nkomo
Vice Chair
Beate Klein Becker Treasurer
Mfundi Vundla Clerk
Janet Axelrod
Toby D'Oench
Melba Kgositsile
Dr. Bernard Magubane
Dr. Renosi Mokate
Geoffrey Norman, Esq.

Themba Vilakazi
Executive Director

Illus: 2.9 - Fund for a Free South Africa • Actual size: 8-7/8" x 3-7/8"

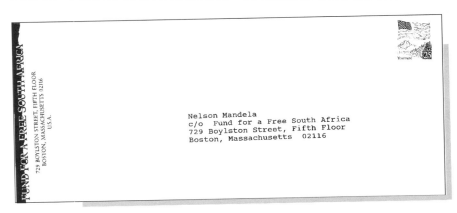

Nelson Mandela
c/o Fund for a Free South Africa
729 Boylston Street, Fifth Floor
Boston, Massachusetts 02116

3

Putting High-Dollar Mail
in its Proper Place

Let's not kid ourselves. Direct mail fundraising, as it has usually been practiced for more than half a century, has developed what might charitably be called certain drawbacks.

Costs have risen dramatically. Skepticism among the public about the efficiency and effectiveness of nonprofit organizations has grown widespread. Competition has increased exponentially, and typical response rates have fallen apace. In addition, public demands for privacy and governmental regulation have limited practitioners' freedom of action.

As a result, direct mail fundraising has long since left behind the days when it was an easy route to a quick buck (as was the case in the halcyon days just after World War II).

In fact, for a great many nonprofit organizations and institutions, a traditional direct mail fundraising program can no longer be fully justified by the immediate rewards it delivers.

In recent decades, most fundraisers have come to accept a new way to view – and justify – the time, talent, and expense invested in direct mail fundraising: the relationship of *Acquisition Cost* and *Long-Term Value*.

When I joined the field in the late 1970s, it was customary to expect that donor-acquisition mailings would break even or, with a bit of luck, turn a modest profit. Some nonprofits are fortunate enough to enjoy such results to this day – but most don't.

The majority of direct mail fundraising programs are characterized by an Acquisition Cost per new donor recruited of anywhere from $1 to $200. (Yes, $200. I've seen it!) There's no excuse for an investment on this scale, sometimes amounting to an annual outlay of $1,000,000 or more for a huge nationwide program, *unless those donors pay off in a very big way*. And they do (usually).

But that payoff is no longer measured simply in terms of the revenue generated by newly acquired donors during the first one, two, or three years after their acquisition – or the second, third, and fourth gifts they might contribute in response to resolicitation mailings.

Nowadays, wise fundraisers look to the Lifetime (or, better put, Long-Term) Value new donors bring to the organization. The Long-Term value includes all of the following:

- Net income from direct mail renewals and special appeals;
- Net income from telefundraising;
- Net income from monthly giving (committed or regular giving) programs;
- Net income from admission fees, merchandise sales, or other fees for goods and services; and,
- Most importantly, net income received over the very long term from major gifts and legacies.

Stacked up against a true Long-Term Value of $100, $200 or more – sometimes much more – an Acquisition Cost of $10 or $20 can look like a very good investment indeed.

But, as direct mail costs and competition continue to rise, how do you increase the Long-Term Value of those donors? How do you identify and cultivate the best candidates for big gifts or legacies? Is old-fashioned direct mail the most suitable technique?

No. And that's the crux of the problem.

Direct mail is traditionally designed to be produced at the lowest possible cost and to deliver impersonal (even if "personalized") messages crafted to match a lowest-common-denominator view of the market.

The result? First-year renewal rates that may range as low as 25%. Donor "lifetimes" of two or three years. Average gifts of $25 or less. And donors who, interviewed in focus groups, don't even recall having contributed to charities they've sent lots of contributions. Are these the makings of major gifts and legacies? I won't insult your intelligence with an answer to that question.

A much broader view of fundraising in general, and of direct mail in particular, is in order.

Start with a donor's-eye-view of fundraising.

Let's say you're one of those people (the overwhelming majority in America, I'm told) who think environmental issues are important. Out of the blue, you receive a direct mail appeal from an activist organization I'll call Green Earth.

On the same day, three other solicitations, two bills, a clothing catalog, and a circular from the local hardware store also show up in your mailbox. But that appeal from Green Earth somehow catches your eye.

You slit it open, skim the contents, note that one of the group's projects relates to a headline story that disturbed you a couple of weeks ago, and you set the appeal aside to respond.

Now, let's assume you're an exceptional person quite unlike the majority of direct mail recipients. The fact that you've snatched that Green Earth appeal out of the day's mail and put it aside immediately establishes how unusual you are, since almost everyone else has unceremoniously tossed it out.

But now you prove you're truly a remarkable person: unlike the estimated 50% of direct mail recipients who set mail aside but never respond, you actually write a check to Green Earth for $30 the next time you pay your bills. That's the amount circled and asterisked on the reply coupon – the amount entitling you to "full membership" in Green Earth, which means you'll receive the newsletter.

You could just as easily send $300 or even $3,000, but they've only asked for $30. Anyway, you know little about the organization except what little you've absorbed in a quick scan of its appeal. You'd need to know more to give a larger gift.

So far, so good. You've identified yourself as a potential donor. Your $30 gift was, really, just a token. But what happens? Green Earth proceeds to treat you as a tried-and-true donor with a deep commitment to its mission.

First you receive a "thank-you" letter suggesting you match your $30 gift and return it in the enclosed Business Reply Envelope – or, better yet, join the Green Earth Sustainers by authorizing the organization to charge $10 "or even $12" per month to your MasterCard.

A couple of weeks later, the first issue of your monthly newsletter arrives, with a remittance envelope tucked inside. Shortly afterward, you receive your first donor appeal, a request for a gift of "$50, $40, or $30" to support Green Earth's campaign to clean up toxic wastes – a program, by the way, that's totally unrelated to the issue that prompted your first gift.

And so it goes for the balance of the year, with newsletters, phone calls, and more straightforward printed fund appeals arriving at intervals of three or four weeks. By the time New Year's rolls around, you're thoroughly disgusted (or at best you've completely lost interest). You wouldn't ever consider making another contribution to Green Earth. Like 75% of the other people who sent first-time gifts, you become a "lapsed member."

Then lo and behold a similar process begins. More newsletters.

More appeals, eventually begging and pleading you not to abandon the Earth to the inevitably horrible fate it will suffer without your continuing active support. But you've long since stopped reading the stuff. And Green Earth may have spent $40 or $50 on communicating with you!

Compare this all-too-typical experience with an alternative approach that builds a long-term relationship with Green Earth *from Dorothy Donor's perspective.* (See the table on the next page.")

Illus: 3.1 - Dorothy Donor's Desire

DOROTHY DONOR'S DESIRE

PROCESS	YOUR ACTIONS	DONOR'S ACTIONS
Identification	Green Earth sends Dorothy a direct mail membership acquisition package	Dorothy identifies herself as a prospective donor by responding with a $30 gift for 'full membership.'
Interest	Green Earth acknowledges Dorothy's initial gift with a warm thank-you and a brief questionnaire asking for information about her interests and communications preferences (phone, email, newsletter) as well as basic demographic and psychographic information.	Dorothy confims her interest by responding to the questionnaire. She declines phone contact and email, and accepts the newsletter. She notes which of Green Earth's issues concern her the most, and expresses the hope she won't be solicited more than twice yearly.
Involvement	Green Earth sends Dorothy its newsletter, a listing of simple actions she can take to respond to the issue she cares most about, and solicits her in the spring and in November	Dorothy skims everything she receives and becomes actively involved in Green Earth's work. At year-end, she sends a $300 gift.
Investment	Green Earth immediately acknowledges Dorothy's dramatic upgrade with a personalized letter and a hand-written postscript – and adds her to the high-dollar cultivation list. She will receive occasional non-solicitation mailings updating her on milestones in the group's work. At the next opportunity, Green Earth invites Dorothy to enroll in its $1,000-a-year giving society, and, over time, gently suggests she consider increasing her support. Once her age is determined, Green Earth will also add her to its legacy-promotion program.	Dorothy continues to pay close attention to the material she receives. The following year, she repeats her $300 gift in the spring – and then, as an initial investment, sends $1,000 at year-end to enlist in the Green Earth high-dollar giving society. Over the years, she gradually increases her annual support from $1,000 to $10,000, even though she insists she doesn't want to be visited by anyone at the organization. Eventually, Dorothy includes Green Earth in her will along with two other charities.

Many fundraisers speak of the Four Phases of Fundraising depicted in Dorothy Donor's Desire. This "Four-I" conceit is merely a mnemonic device that helps to slice and dice the long-term relationships that fundraisers speak of so fondly (but so often fail to achieve, especially if they use direct mail extensively).

There are other ways to characterize the fundraising process, and many other terms. Some place these stages in a different order. But most of us who attempt to reduce to simple categories the admittedly complex and varied experience of the fundraising process come up with something much like the following four phases:

• *Identification*, in which the organization identifies and recruits a first-time donor;

• *Interest*, during which the organization cultivates the donor's interest by providing additional information about its work and its mission;

• *Involvement*, the process of persuading the donor to play a larger role in the work of the organization than merely making occasional cash contributions; and

• *Investment*, when the donor comes to accept the organization and its work as an integral part of her life and makes one or more significant investments in it, either in the form of major gifts or of a legacy.

When you approach these Four Phases in a donor-centric manner, as Dorothy Donor would have you do, you'll master the process and maximize your donors' Long-Term Value.

High-dollar direct mail is an integral and essential element in that process – and I've chosen the words "integral" and "essential" advisedly. Integral, in the sense that, from the donors' point of view, the process is seamless. And essential, because high-dollar direct mail forms *the bridge that links your membership or small-donor program with your work to encourage major gifts and legacies*. That's the special role high-dollar direct mail fundraising plays in the overall development program.

Of course, implementing a high-dollar direct mail effort in the seamless fashion I'm describing is easier said than done. Your development program must be truly donor-ready.

Far too many nonprofit board members and executives assume they can start raising big gifts as soon as the ink on their budgets is dry. Not so. Donors, especially major donors, can smell a lack of readiness for fundraising a mile away.

To approach them with any hope of tapping their generosity, you have to be able to demonstrate a track record of success, a powerful case for giving, an ability to steward gifts successfully, opportunities for designated gifts and corresponding recognition, and the leadership necessary to make all the pieces fit together.

A high-dollar direct mail fundraising program can only be built on such a base – but even that's not enough to ensure its success. At a bare minimum, you'll also need the following:

• You must be prepared to take the long view, looking on your work as an effort to build Long-Term Value and spending the necessary money to educate, involve, and cultivate your donors.

• Your membership or direct marketing department must be on such good terms with the staff who manage your major donor and legacy work that they'll actively cooperate in maximizing contributions from each donor and, where appropriate, following up directly with responsive individuals.

• Your donor acknowledgement process must be both speedy and flexible. It's no use sending out elaborate high-dollar appeals and then failing to thank the donors who respond in anything less than an exemplary fashion – and without delay.

If you can manage all that – no small feat – you'll be well on your way to building a productive high-dollar direct mail fundraising program.

However, first you'll have to determine which of your donors are appropriate prospects, what case for giving is the most likely to unlock their generosity, and what package formats and designs are best calculated to ensure that your appeals will be read. Those topics are covered in the following chapter, "This is not your grandfather's direct mail."

This is Not Your Grandfather's Direct Mail

When I'm asked how high-dollar direct mail differs from garden-variety direct mail, I'm always tempted to say "in every possible way." But it's more accurate to say that there are four distinct dimensions in which the two approaches diverge: (1) in who the letters are sent to; (2) in the case for giving; (3) in the packaging; and (4) in the follow-up. Let's take a look at each of those four dimensions in turn.

■ The list of prospects or donors must be painstakingly chosen.

Time for a pop quiz.

Which of the following would you include in an invitation to join a $1,000-a-year annual giving society? (Select any that apply.)

A) Donors who have contributed one or more individual gifts of $250 – 999 during the past three years.

B) Donors who have contributed two or more individual gifts of $100 – 999 during the past three years.

C) Donors who contributed $1,000 – 4,999 at some time in the past but have not given during the past year.

If you selected (A), (B), *and* (C), go to the head of the class. Your answer might not make everyone happy, but you're clearly on the right track.

Some people would question whether donors of as little as $100 should be included in mailings that might cost $5 or more per piece. Others might contest the inclusion of any donor who has ever given more than $1,000 in a mailing that asks for only that amount (which is something I would only do with lapsed $1,000+ donors.) But I've produced strong results using all three criteria. If you doubt that, take another look at the results reported at the beginning of Chapter 1.

Ideally, grouping all these segments together, you'll muster a list of at least 1,000 high-dollar giving club prospects. With one thousand – or, better yet, several thousand – you'll gain enough economies of scale in production to keep the unit cost somewhere within the bounds of acceptance.

The temptation will probably be strong to drive the unit cost even lower by including a number of prospective donors in the appeal. You might consider any or all of the following possible sources of additional high-dollar donors:

• Donors of amounts of less than $100 identified by a wealth-screening service as having the capacity to give much larger gifts;

• Prospects suggested by members of your board of directors or other well-connected people who have personal knowledge of the giving habits and capacity of donors to other organizations;

• Members of a high-prestige profession such as medicine or the law that is integrally related to your mission (healthcare or civil rights, for example);

• Names selected by a list broker from commercially available lists of "millionaires" identified through wealth-screening or geodemographic methods; or

• Names of $100+ direct-mail-acquired donors obtained through a name-for-name exchange with a like-minded nonprofit organization (or as a favor for one-time usage).

Under varying circumstances, my colleagues and I have tested lists in all these categories over the years. Results have been decidedly mixed. Only one category has worked consistently well: high-dollar direct-mail-acquired donors provided, usually on exchange, by another nonprofit. Lists of professionals or "millionaires" have almost always performed poorly.

Now, you may be tempted, if you're going to all this trouble, to "throw in" some or even all the rest of your donors, in the belief that a larger quantity will help you lower the unit cost of the mailing. But this would be a mistake. An offer tailored to high-dollar donors is likely to be ineffective with donors who habitually give less than $100.

■ The case for giving must be compelling and tailored to high-dollar donors.

In direct mail, the case for giving is built around an "offer" – a marketing concept that conveys how much money the signer wants the reader to send and what the gift will accomplish. Most traditional direct mail fundraising offers fall into one or another of the following four types:

A) "Send $25 now, and we'll save the life of this [*select one*: child, small furry animal, adorable major mammal, starving person, natural wonder]."

B) "With your $25 contribution, we can continue the great progress we've made in the fight [for/against] [fill-in-the-blank]."

C) "Your $25 gift will remove the object of your [*select one*: fear, guilt, shame, doubt, etc.]."

D) "If you send us $25, we'll guarantee that [the ideal you hold most dearly] is kept alive in the hearts and minds of humankind."

Now, for just a moment, step out of your fundraiser's skin and apply the B.S. test to these four propositions. Could you stand face-to-face with anyone over the age of six and say any of these things with a straight face? And do you think *for even one second* that any serious person would respond to an appeal of this sort if you asked for $1,000 instead of $25?

I'm going to assume your answers to those questions are the same as mine, okay? Let's move on, then.

With a little bit of careful thought, we can imagine what sorts of offers might be taken more seriously. This line of thinking will lead us into an examination of donor motivation – the real reasons people respond to fundraising appeals.

Traditionalists in the field of direct marketing speak about five "hot buttons" or "triggers" that explain donor motivation (just as they allegedly explain buyers' behavior): *fear, guilt, greed, exclusivity,* and *anger*.

These base emotions lie at the heart of the offers that dominate direct mail fundraising today, as you can easily deduce through a quick re-reading of the four stereotypical approaches I listed above.

To some degree, one or another of these five emotions is probably associated with almost any offer we might imagine. But I regard this approach as simplistic and misleading.

The human psyche is far more complex than any five-point typology would suggest. And *positive* emotions can be just as powerful as negative ones.

In fact, marketing research makes clear that religious or spiritual values are among the most compelling drivers of philanthropic behavior – not just in North America, where the research has been most extensive, but all across the globe.

After all, every major spiritual tradition – Islam, Hinduism, Buddhism, Judaism, and Christianity – lays great emphasis on sharing and generosity. Philanthropy is universal, though it may take different forms from one culture to another. Surely, the universality of giving behavior alone suggests that positive emotions must play a role in fundraising!

In fact, I believe there are five positive triggers that just as often play key roles in motivating donors to give: *hope, love, faith, duty,* and *compassion*. In the context of this book, it's critical to recognize that positive emotions such as these are even more likely to figure prominently in high-dollar appeals than they do in traditional direct mail.

Consider some of the more obvious demographic and lifestyle characteristics we can deduce about typical high-dollar donors:

• They have sufficient cash available to be able to make spontaneous gifts of $1,000 or more at a time. Most likely, then, they're high-salaried professionals or executives, successful small businesspeople, remarkably successful artists or freelancers, heirs to wealth or beneficiaries of trust funds – or drug dealers. (Few of the latter, however, are noted for their philanthropic orientation toward the world.)

• Such people tend to be unusually busy, with multiple demands on their time and many competing claims on their generosity. A significant proportion of them review their mail only after an assistant or a secretary opens and screens it first.

• Chances are, they're older than the median age – 40s, 50s, 60s, and older, and thus in what is increasingly called "the second half of life." Unlike younger donors, many retain some degree of faith in existing institutions. They're skeptical about careless claims, but less cynical than their children and grandchildren.

• Like direct mail donors in general, they tend to be college-educated. Many possess advanced degrees. They've learned the habits of critical thinking. They often read widely and are well-informed.

• They're commonly involved in their communities, often deeply. A majority regularly attend religious services. They vote.

The work of the pioneering psychologist, Abraham Maslow, helps to cast additional light on donor motivation. Maslow wrote about the hierarchy of human needs, describing our emotional development through life as following an upward progression from the most basic to the most refined.

At the base of Maslow's hierarchy lie our *physiological* needs – for food, sex, and shelter. Next up the ladder is our need for *safety*. Then comes *belonging*, which is only possible if our more basic needs have first been met. Esteem lies higher on the ladder. The final stage in our emotional development is the need for *self-actualization*, that state of fulfillment at which we truly encompass our interdependence with the world around us.

As you can see, charitable giving of the more meaningful sort represented by gifts of $1,000 or more isn't likely at any of the three bottom-most levels of Maslow's hierarchy, which are concerned with the needs of the self.

Giving can be – and sometimes is – one way in which we display our craving for esteem. Hence, "donor recognition." But true philanthropy, the love of humankind, becomes habitual only once we have achieved a level of emotional maturity that enables us to feel genuine empathy.

We needn't make any unwarranted assumptions about the emotional maturity of high-dollar donors (which would, of course, be highly debatable). But surely we can agree that few if any of these individuals or their loved ones are likely to experience urgent needs for physical survival, personal safety, or even a sense that they have no place in the world.

Chances are, their motives for giving will tend to be more complex than simple anger, fear, guilt, greed, or exclusivity.

If you appeal to your donors' best instincts, you'll find that they're just as interested as you are in making the world a better place for all.

Research into donor motivation repeatedly demonstrates that donors – not just high-dollar donors, but most donors – give in response to nonprofits' *vision* and *mission*. Because, after all, your vision and mission point to the way you're helping improve the quality of life on earth.

Taking into account the probable profile of high dollar donors, here are five alternative approaches you might take in crafting a high-dollar case for giving:

• "[This situation] confronts us with a challenge—and an opportunity—of historic proportions. The Board of Trustees has therefore decided to launch [the Campaign for X] – an effort of truly unprecedented scope and intensity. This campaign will represent our very highest priority for at least the next three years. I invite you to help us get this extraordinary effort off the ground by enrolling as a Charter Sponsor with a commitment to contribute at least $1,000 per year."

• "I hope we can count on you and other loyal and generous donors to contribute a minimum of $1,000 per year. Only then can my staff and I lay our plans for the years ahead with sufficient assurance that we will have the resources to confront [these critical challenges I've just mentioned]."

• "Foundations and other institutional supporters provide xx% of our funding, but we must turn to generous individuals like you to supply the balance. And institutional support is typically designated for specific projects, leaving me and my staff without the funds we need to sustain our operations from day to day. Your commitment to contribute a minimum of $1,000 per year will help close the gap."

• "Our operating budget prepares us for the future we know – but there is so much we don't know. Your annual gift of $1,000 or more will provide the funding we need to meet unanticipated challenges and capitalize on unexpected opportunities."

• "As one of our most loyal and generous donors, I'm sure you're aware that the challenge we face is more daunting than ever. That's why I'm calling on you and a few other individuals who have demonstrated true leadership in the past to help underwrite our ambitious new campaign with a gift of $1,000 or more per year."

If any starving children or desperate little animals figure into any of these offers, they take a back seat to the lofty ideals represented by the organizations' vision and mission – the Big Picture ideas and ideals that light donors' hearts afire – *even if they revolve around a specific issue or project.*

These examples by no means constitute a comprehensive list. They merely suggest a broad range of possible approaches to crafting a case for giving that's suitable for high-dollar donors.

If you pursue a line of argument somewhat like one of these, and if you've chosen the right list of prospects, you'll be that much closer to success in your high-dollar direct mail fundraising program. But one critical area of concern remains to be considered: the format and design of your high-dollar package.

■ The appeal must be packaged in a truly engaging way.

Which of the following methods do you use to sort the mail when you return from a vacation or a business trip?

1) Immediately discard anything that's not personally addressed to you.

2) Set aside anything that looks interesting or important and toss out the rest.

3) Put all first-class mail in one stack and "junk mail" in another (to be glanced at casually if you have the time and the inclination sometime later).

4) Separate the mail into four piles: bills, personal mail (if any), solicitations, and commercial advertising matter.

No matter which approach you (or your high-dollar prospects) might follow, your high-dollar package needs to stand out enough to be selected *in* to the pile that actually gets read. It must appear to be personally addressed. It must have an air of importance about it. And it must bear first-class postage (preferably live postage stamps).

Forget the trappings of standard direct mail: the lurid teasers, the bulk rate postage, the raggedy ink-jet addressing systems, the barcodes, the window envelopes, the cheap 50-pound paper stock. High-dollar direct mail packages must avoid the look and feel of junk mail at all costs. They must be *distinctive*.

Illus: 4.1 - Aids Project Los Angeles • Actual size: 12" x 9"

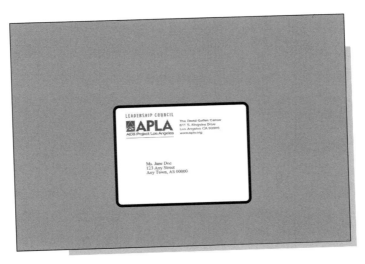

As a practical matter, this will usually mean that your package must incorporate all of the following elements:

• An oversized carrier envelope (7-1/2" x 10-1/2", 9" x 12", 9-1/2" x 12-1/2", or something similar) constructed from high-quality, usually laid-finish (textured) paper stock, perhaps even brightly colored;

• First-class postage stamps that are hand-affixed and include at least one colorful commemorative;

• Addressing, whether by laser-printer or by hand, that appears to have been done by a human being;

• High-quality paper stock for all package contents, ideally linen or matching laid-finish stock;

• Personalization on both the letter and the reply device to match that on the carrier; and

• A reply envelope bearing a first-class stamp (or no postage at all) – but *not* a Business Reply Envelope.

Ready now? Do you have all your ducks lined up in a row: targeting, messaging, and packaging? Terrific! Now the real work begins.

■ You must follow up – and follow through!

Think about the four-phase fundraising process I described in Chapter 3. Reread that section, if necessary. It won't take more than a few seconds' reflection to realize that a high-dollar mailing of the sort I've been describing would be only marginally useful as a one-shot proposition.

Oh, sure, you might be able to upgrade a significant number of your donors and realize a substantial profit. Chances are, you'd receive phone calls and letters from a few of your donors, perhaps including members of your board, who are impressed with the letters you've sent. (If you do your job well, you're bound to receive such comments from people who've always *detested* direct mail.)

But if you merely send out a simple high-dollar mailing once every year or so, you'll be squandering the true value of high-dollar direct mail fundraising. Keep in mind that, from a strategic perspective, high-dollar direct mail is a way for you to bridge the gap between the small-donor world and the realm of major gifts.

Functionally, high-dollar mail needs to serve as a communications platform to upgrade the most promising candidates from your small-donor program to a level of giving that's high enough to warrant attention from major gifts staff and volunteers. That requires a continuing program – a fundraising track of its own, really.

And like any well-managed fundraising track – membership, major gifts, legacies, whatever – a high-dollar fundraising program consists of at least the following elements:

- Gift acknowledgements;
- Cultivation, education, and reporting;
- Annual renewal efforts; and
- Special appeals.

Every one of these efforts must be conceived and managed with a view toward the special needs, preferences, and circumstances of high-dollar donors. For example, it's a mistake to include such donors in a standard annual renewal series or in traditional special appeals – even if the immediate result might well be to turn a substantial profit. Keep your eye on the long haul, and your rewards over time will be even greater.

I'll discuss each of these elements in some detail in Chapter 6, "Bringing your high-dollar program to life." Meanwhile, I'd like you to join me in the following chapter on "A guided tour through a contemporary high-dollar appeal."

A Guided Tour Through a Contemporary High-Dollar Appeal

If I've made anything clear so far in this book, I hope I've convinced you that high-dollar mail looks and feels very different from traditional direct mail. Such old-standby techniques as window envelopes, inkjet addressing, and outer envelope teasers are all no-nos. In the parlance of the computer industry, the "look and feel" of a high-dollar mailing needs to convey a sense of gravity consistent with the appeal's lofty language.

So it was with the high-dollar invitation package mailed by *Riverkeeper* (Garrison, New York) that appears in these pages. Riverkeeper is an advocacy group that has been monitoring the Hudson River ecosystem and challenging polluters, using both legal and grassroots campaigns, since the 1960s.

It was the inspiration for more than 125 local and regional

"waterkeeper" organizations that have been established under names such as "Riverkeeper," "Lakekeeper," "Baykeeper," and "Coastkeeper" all across the United States and in half a dozen other countries.

Illus: 5.1 - Riverkeeper • Actual size: 12" x 9"

• *The carrier envelope*

This invitation to enroll in Riverkeeper's Hudson River Stewards Club was mailed in an unprinted (blank) gray 12" x 9" envelope. The envelope bore a large, hand-affixed, pressure-sensitive mailing label printed in dark blue and addressed on a laser printer. A first-class stamp featuring an environmental theme appeared in the upper right-hand corner, bearing sufficient postage to cover the mailing cost at the two-ounce rate.

Illus: 5.2 - Riverkeeper • Actual size: 8-1/2" x 11"

P.O. Box 130
Garrison, NY 10524
www.riverkeeper.org

RIVERKEEPER.

Hudson River Stewards

March 25, 2004

Ms. Jane Doe
123 Any Street
Anytown, AS 00000

Dear Ms. Doe,

Looking out my office window, I see the snow is melting off the fields outside and the ice has started to break up on the Hudson River. But here in Highlands, we are still playing host to about 100 wintering bald eagles. Yesterday, near the water's edge, I watched about 25 of these majestic birds fishing on the ice flows.

That sight made me think about how 30 years ago, due to pollution and DDT use, we only had 425 nesting pairs of eagles in the entire lower 48 states. Now, thanks to the efforts of people like you, the bald eagle and other wildlife have been brought back from the brink of extinction. Thanks to all our efforts, the Hudson River valley is once again becoming a place of natural beauty and vibrant communities.

As one of Riverkeeper's most generous and loyal supporters, you are an integral part of an incredibly successful effort to restore and protect one of America's greatest natural treasures.

What 40 years of fighting for the Hudson River has taught us is that this work requires <u>constant vigilance</u>. But when we reflect on the near-devastation and redemption of the Hudson River over the last 40 years, I think you'll agree, we must commit ourselves to nothing less.

I'm writing today to ask you to help launch *The Hudson River Stewards Club*, an exciting new initiative to ensure that Riverkeeper has the resources available to draw on the wide range of expertise needed to protect the Hudson River, its valley, and the surrounding communities.

I am pleased to invite you to become a key participant in this new endeavor by becoming a Charter Member with a contribution of $10,000 or more.

This request may strike you as large, as indeed it is, but as one of Riverkeeper's key supporters, you know how great our success can be. And you understand the urgency and complexity of our efforts to eliminate current threats and meet new challenges.

Together, the members of *The Hudson River Stewards Club* will underwrite Riverkeeper's powerful collaborations among scientists, lawyers, community activists, and experts in a wide array of fields.

I'm sure you agree that people's rights and the sanctity of the natural environment must always be balanced. By joining *The Hudson River Stewards Club* now, you will help ensure that they never again collide in the near disaster that the Hudson River once faced.

• *The letter*

The first thing the recipient was likely to notice on opening this package was the paper clip affixed (by hand, of course) to the upper

Illus: 5.3 - Riverkeeper

This commitment to balance—and to real, workable solutions—has been the hallmark of Riverkeeper's past success.

Your leadership support now is key to the river's future—as the threats to the river continue to become more numerous, more varied, and, in many ways, more complex.

By joining *The Hudson River Stewards Club* now, you are enabling Riverkeeper to address these new threats facing the river from pollution to over-development.

Environmental scientists and legal advocates have always been at the core of Riverkeeper's work. But more and more, we must also draw on the knowledge and advice of energy specialists, land use planners, economists, public health monitors, and countless other experts.

Then we must synthesize all this information to develop viable, long-lasting solutions. And we must build and strengthen the citizens' movement to make those solutions a reality.

I hope I can count on you to join me in meeting this historic challenge.

As I travel up and down the river, I see firsthand the results of the important work we do together. Fish life is thriving. Migrating and nesting birds are returning. Native wetland plants are proliferating. More and more people are swimming, fishing, boating, and enjoying the river—without harming it. And, most basic of all, the water is cleaner and clearer.

I am deeply grateful for your partnership in this work, and I hope you'll take a very significant step forward by becoming a Charter Member of *The Hudson River Stewards Club* today.

When you join, you will receive a signed copy of the book *The Riverkeepers* and invitations to special events. Your membership will be recognized in the Riverkeeper Annual Report and at the Annual Gala next month. From time to time, you will be invited to attend personal meetings with Riverkeeper leaders.

Most importantly, as a new generation of activists carries the torch of Hudson River protection, you'll know that you are playing a leadership role in continuing one of our nation's most remarkable environmental success stories.

Working together we can bring state-of-the-art knowledge and analysis to bear on our critical efforts to protect the Hudson. We will continually develop innovative solutions, staying flexible and creative enough to respond to ever-changing political and environmental conditions.

Membership in *The Hudson River Stewards Club* is truly a remarkable gift to the river and the surrounding valley, to all the plant and animal life that depends on these resources, and to all those who benefit from the beauty and bounty for generations to come.

I thank you in advance for your commitment and your vision.

Sincerely,

Alex Matthiessen
Riverkeeper & Executive Director

P.S.　Thank you for considering this very important request. And, if you haven't been to the river lately, I hope you'll make plans to come soon. Please consider a trip to the Riverkeeper office and ride with me on the river so I can show you how you are making such a critical difference in the life of this remarkable waterway.

left-hand corner of the letter. This clip fastened the letter to the "proposal" described below, lending a touch of human intervention that reinforced the impression this appeal was mailed by a human being, not a machine.

On simple, unadorned letterhead printed on high-quality cream stock, this high-dollar giving society invitation gave readers the appearance of serious correspondence from Alex Matthiessen, Riverkeeper's Executive Director.

Note the language of the initial paragraphs, which grounded readers in the sensitive worldview of an organization that had labored for more than a third of a century to restore and preserve the beauty of the Hudson River Valley.

As the text made clear (in the third paragraph), this invitation was mailed to many of Riverkeeper's "most generous and loyal supporters." The letter announced the formation of The Hudson River Stewards Club, a six-tiered annual giving society with giving opportunities all the way from $1,000 to $100,000 per year.

The particular letter illustrated here requested a Charter Membership gift of $10,000 or $20,000. Other letters suggested lower amounts. None was higher.

Note the repeated use of such phrases as "key participant," "leadership support," "partnership" and "leadership role," and the closing reference to "your commitment and your vision." In all these and other ways, this appeal was squarely targeted at older donors who were experiencing what Maslow termed self-actualization.

Normally, my colleagues and I do not print high-dollar letters back to back, as this letter was printed. However, as an environmental organization highly conscious of resource use, Riverkeeper opted to do so.

The letter was hand-signed on behalf of Alex Matthiessen.

• *The brochure*

As you can see on the next several pages, Riverkeeper did not enclose any ordinary brochure in its initial high-dollar invitation. This

Illus: 5.4 - Riverkeeper • Actual size: 8-1/2" x 11"

Illus: 5.5 - Riverkeeper

I. Hudson River Stewards

The Hudson is a world-class river. It travels over 300 miles from its source in the Adirondacks through the Appalachian Mountains in the Hudson Highlands, and into 150 miles of tidal estuary to the mouth of New York Harbor. The river is known for its vast ecological diversity, for its place in American history, and for its sheer beauty. It is the lifeblood of the region. Once highly polluted, the Hudson River has experienced a remarkable recovery in the past 30 years, rebounding from decades of neglect and abuse.

As Riverkeeper celebrates its 40 years of restoring and protecting the Hudson River, the necessity of developing viable solutions based on the knowledge and advice of multiple experts is key to the river's future. Riverkeeper has launched *The Hudson River Stewards Club* to ensure that the necessary resources are available when needed to overcome the multiple threats to the river and its surroundings. You are invited to play an instrumental role in this historic venture as a Charter Member.

Hudson River Stewards will make an annual commitment of $1,000 or more to underwrite the expertise required to protect the Hudson River and its communities. Charter Membership Giving Levels include the following benefits and privileges:

Hudson River Stewards: Annual Contribution of $1,000–$4,999

- Autographed copy of *The Riverkeepers* by John Cronin and Robert Kennedy, Jr.
- Recognition in the Riverkeeper Annual Report and Annual Gala Program
- Invitation to Special Events
- Special updates on programs and current events

Hudson River Falcons: Annual Contribution of $5,000–$9,999

All of the above, plus...
- Special invitations to strategy sessions with Riverkeeper leaders on the critical issues facing the Hudson River and its valley

Hudson River Eagles: Annual contribution of $10,000–$19,999

All of the above, plus...
- Exclusive participation in River Patrols with the Hudson Riverkeeper

Protectors of the Hudson: Annual contribution of $20,000–$49,999

All of the above, plus...
- Invitations to participate in ground-breaking research trips conducted by Riverkeeper and a team of renowned researchers

Storm King Guardians: Annual contribution of $50,000–$99,0000

All of the above, plus...
- Invitations to intimate presentations and events with Riverkeeper leaders and renowned supporters
- Priority seating for two at Riverkeeper events, including the 2005 Annual Gala

Illus: 5.6 - Riverkeeper

Tear of the Clouds Circle

All of the above, plus...

◆ Table for ten guests at the 2005 Annual Gala including special recognition at the event and in the dinner program

II. Riverkeeper Priorities and the Role of Key Experts

• Stopping Pollution of the River

Citizen enforcement brings environmental lawbreakers to justice, and Riverkeeper serves as the Hudson River's chief citizen-based pollution enforcement organization. Investigations and cases usually start with a simple phone call, an e-mail, or someone hailing down our patrol boat out on the river. Our boat captain, John Lipscomb, may investigate the issue himself or call into the office for support. At any given time, Riverkeeper is usually involved in 35 to 40 federal or state cases. Once we enter a case, we have to assemble a team of experts including attorneys, engineers, biologists, hydrologists, economists, and energy policy analysts.

Costs for current and upcoming cases: $475,000

• Fighting Damaging Development and Sprawl

Pollution caused by overdevelopment threatens to reverse recent gains in water quality and destroy community character along the Hudson River and its surrounding valley. A core component of our program is monitoring and reviewing proposed development projects. To do this, we must work with developers, government officials, and coalition to practice and promote smart growth and low impact development.

We engage land use planners, traffic engineers, and regulatory, legislative, and environmental impact analysts to develop solutions that balance the needs of industry, local communities, and the river.

Cost for 2004: $312,000

• Shutting Down Indian Point Nuclear Reactors

Over the last two years, Riverkeeper has taken what once seemed an impossible goal—shutting down the Indian Point nuclear reactors—and turned it into a major issue for tl New York metropolitan area. To date, more than 40 municipalities, 200 elected official several school boards, community groups, and labor unions have called for the shutdov of the plants.

Riverkeeper has spearheaded the effort to inform the public about the dangers of a terrorist attack on the plant.

Illus: 5.7 - Riverkeeper

Riverkeeper must continually consult with energy experts to analyze the region's energy needs and determine the consequences of decommissioning the plants, in order to develop a blueprint for plant closing that takes into account concerns about energy supply and pricing, jobs, and the tax base.

Cost for 2004: $180,000

- **Cleaning up GE PCBs**

From 1947 to 1977, General Electric dumped an estimated 13 million tons of PCBs into the river from its two Hudson River manufacturing plants. PCBs are an industrial chemical, especially toxic to aquatic life. PCBs accumulate potency as they work their way up the food chain, and they have been linked to cancer and reproductive and developmental disorders in people.

Riverkeeper and its alliance of environmental groups are determined to continue to apply pressure on GE until the company commits itself to financing and expeditiously executing the full EPA cleanup plan.

To keep the pressure on GE and the EPA to proceed quickly with the most thorough and effective clean up, Riverkeeper must draw on the expertise of hydrologists, engineers, environmental health specialists, aquatic biologists, and regulatory experts.

Cost for 2004: $74,000

III. The Solution

The establishment of *The Hudson River Stewards Club* will enable Riverkeeper to draw on the expertise required *at the crucial moments we need it most* to achieve major legal, political, and environmental victories for the river and surrounding communities. We need to engage our committed partners to raise $1,041,000 for our work this year. *The Hudson River Stewards* will provide leadership fundamental to the long-term dreams and responsibilities of all those who care deeply about the future of the river.

> If we don't all stand up and defend our right to protect that waterway, we'll lose both the waterway and our right to protect it. The only way to win a battle is to fight it. You will most certainly lose every battle you don't fight.
>
> — *John Cronin, former commercial fisherman and the nation's first Riverkeeper, serving the Hudson community from 1983 to 2000*

RIK4-AA5

63

four-page document was couched as "A Proposal from Alex Matthiessen, Hudson Riverkeeper and Executive Director, Prepared for (Jane Doe)"

This proposal, reminiscent of major gift proposals tailored to the interests of individual donors, described the benefits associated with each of the six contribution levels and made the case for giving by assigning estimated costs for each of four priority areas of activity.

Significantly, the proposal closed by saying "The establishment of The Hudson River Stewards Club will enable Riverkeeper to draw on the expertise required at the crucial moments we need it most ...." This wording confirmed that gifts would be undesignated by area of activity – a significant advantage to the organization.

After all, from a management standpoint, one of the greatest virtues of individual support from members or donors is that it is typically undesignated. Although most major donor fundraising focuses on earmarked gifts, *high-dollar fundraising can be successfully conducted without the need to do so.*

• *The response device*

Several aspects of the "Memorandum of Acceptance" on the facing page are worthy of special note:

• Personalization appeared not just in the "FROM" field at the top but also in the message area below – and in the suggested levels of giving, which varied with individual donor history.

• As in any well-crafted direct mail response device, the language that appeared after "Dear Alex" restated the benefits detailed in the package.

• To encourage repeat giving even if the donor rejected the sort of dramatic upgrade this package sought, the response device offered the recipient the opportunity to contribute a smaller amount.

• A signature line subtly reinforced the commitment that the appeal sought from donors and provided a subtle involvement opportunity.

• In the space at the bottom of the page, the donor had the opportunity to spell out his name for listing in the Riverkeeper annual

Illus: 5.8 - Riverkeeper • Actual size: 8-1/2" x 11"

MEMORANDUM OF ACCEPTANCE

TO: Alex Matthiessen
Riverkeeper & Executive Director

Hudson River Stewards

FROM: Ms. Jane Doe
123 Any Street
Anytown, AS 00000

0
04AA-DOE

RIVERKEEPER,

CC: Robert F. Kennedy, Chief Prosecuting Attorney

25 Wing & Wing
Garrison, NY 10524-9910
845-424-4149
www.riverkeeper.org

ABOUT: **The Hudson River Stewards Club Charter Membership**

Dear Alex,

I'm very pleased to accept your invitation to play a leadership role ensuring the birthright of all the Hudson River's inhabitants to enjoy its immense beauty and bounty today and for future generations. Please enroll me as a Charter Member of *The Hudson River Stewards Club* to help bring state-of-the-art knowledge and analysis to bear on all our critical efforts to protect the river.

I understand that as a **Charter Member of *The Hudson River Stewards Club*** I will receive a signed copy of *The Riverkeepers*, recognition in the Riverkeeper Annual Report and at the Annual Gala, invitations to special events, and personal meetings with Riverkeeper leaders.

Please enroll me as a Hudson River Steward at the level indicated below:

[ ] $10,000

I'm interested in an expanded role in Riverkeeper. I'm enrolling at the following level:

[ ] Protectors of the Hudson $20,000*

*Eligible for additional benefits, as indicated in the enclosed proposal.

[ ] I am unable to join *The Hudson River Stewards Club* at this time. Please accept my gift of $_____.

Signed: _____   _____
Ms. Jane Doe   Date

☐ Please list my (our) name(s) in the Riverkeeper Annual Report as follows:

_____

☐ I prefer that my gift remain anonymous.

☐ My check to Riverkeeper is enclosed.   ☐ Please charge my *(circle one)* VISA/MC/Amex

Card # _____ Exp. Date _____

Your contribution is tax-deductible to the full extent of the law. Thank you for your commitment and your vision.

RIK4-AA2

report or to stipulate that it remain anonymous. At higher giving levels, many donors are uneasy about having their names publicly revealed.

Illus: 5.9 - Riverkeeper • Actual Size: 8-7/8" x 3-7/8"

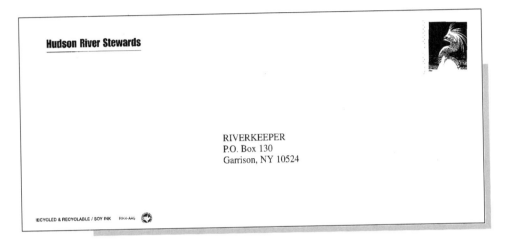

• *The reply envelope*

This white, #9 reply envelope, pre-addressed to Riverkeeper, bore a first-class stamp that, like the one on the carrier envelope, featured an environmental theme. Happily, the bird image on this stamp matched the theme of the letter's opening, which was about birds on the Hudson.

The printed word and black-and-white illustrations can't communicate the impact such a package might have on a typical high-dollar donor. Still, I hope that viewing this appeal up close helps to give you a sense of the dynamics at work in the process.

As you move along to Chapter 6, "Bringing your high-dollar program to life," keep in mind the upscale impression this appeal conveys. That will help you understand the bigger picture we're now about to explore.

Bringing Your High-Dollar Program to Life

Think about Dorothy Donor and her high expectations of prompt and personalized service. If you've been raising money for more than a short time, I'm sure you'll recognize that Dorothy is hardly exceptional in that regard. After all, most of us would like to think that we'll be treated as human beings rather than statistics! And it's that simple precept on which donor-centered fundraising is based.

■ Put high-dollar donors at the center of your universe.

This is the part where you have to bend your mind in unfamiliar ways.

For starters, take a look at the illustration on the next page labeled "The Traditional Direct Mail Universe."

Admit it now. You practically have to run a gantlet to make contact with the donors or members who are supposedly the reason for your professional existence.

The Traditional Direct Mail Universe

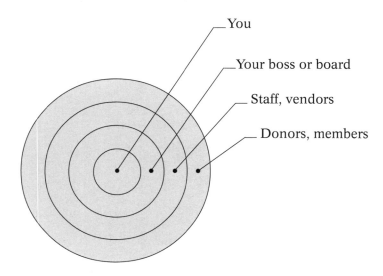

First you've got to get by your boss or the board, who will let you do some things but not others. Then you've got to wrestle with your colleagues, staff, vendors, or consultants to craft the communications that will help you reach out to your donors. Finally, you reach the outer stretches of your universe and – every once in a while – achieve contact and gain understanding.

If this isn't true about your situation, you're an exception. Most of us are caught up in the often petty realities of everyday life. We're hemmed in by laws, regulations, rules, traditions, beliefs, values, customs, budgets – and the maddeningly complex ways of human relations. Free will? In a philosopher's dream, maybe. If only everybody would just go away and leave us alone!

But you don't have to take it lying down. There *is* another way. It will require considerable leadership on your part – mostly gumption and stick-to-itiveness – and you'll have to bring your colleagues along. You can't pull this off alone.

But if you begin with the premise that *your organization can accomplish absolutely nothing without the generous, ongoing support of its donors* ... if you recognize that you and your colleagues are dispensable, but your donors aren't ... and if you follow that logic through to its inevitable conclusion ... then you'll realize that you've been operating in an upside-down or inside-out fashion for far too long.

To glimpse the way things ought to be, contrast "The Traditional Direct Mail Universe" with "The Donor-Centered Universe."

The Donor-Centered Universe

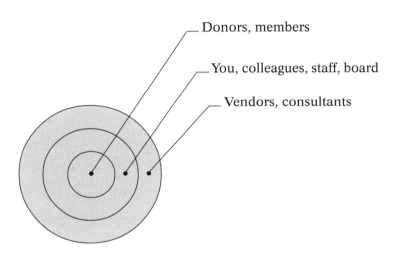

Donors, members

You, colleagues, staff, board

Vendors, consultants

I can hear you now. You're saying "Okay, this is cute, but what does it really mean? As a practical matter, what can I do to put in place a donor-centered fundraising program?"

Read on. In the following sections, I'll spell out precisely what I mean by a donor-centered fundraising program – one that will be especially effective in warming the hearts of your high-dollar donors.

In fact, ideally, you would implement a similar approach with *all* your donors.

■ Cultivate high-dollar donors, and provide them with meaningful opportunities for involvement.

In a donor-centered program, you would at the very least take the following steps to involve and cultivate your donors:

• Send a warm, distinctive thank-you immediately after you receive every gift.

• Make sure some of your mailings are for information only – *not* solicitations.

• Survey your donors from time to time about their views and preferences. Listen well and bide by their preferences. This is not a marketing ploy.

• Ask what communications your donors wish to receive from you, and through which channels (mail, telephone, email, etc.) – and follow their wishes.

• Ask how frequently they wish to be solicited – and comply!

• Offer your donors any and all appropriate means to become more meaningfully involved in your work, whether as advisors, visitors, volunteers, trustees, or through special events or issue briefings.

Throughout this book, I've talked about how your organization can create mailings that prompt donors to send you gifts of $1,000 – or even more. One of the most important reasons such mailings work is that many of those who respond to direct mail are well-to-do – even though they may send you checks of just $50, $25 (or even less!). Indeed, many of your "low-dollar" donors are making four and five-figure gifts to other organizations.

The potential of tapping great wealth, and a pattern of generous giving by many high-dollar donors, suggest that an effective high-dollar fundraising program must consist of more than just a single appeal mailing.

Rather, it must encompass a carefully planned sequence of communications that will give your donors enough information so they understand *why* your organization needs gifts of $1,000 or more. With the right mix of mailings over the course of an entire year, you also communicate a level of appreciation and trustworthiness that inspires such gifts.

To give you a clearer picture of how a donor-centered high-dollar fundraising program calculated to tap this wealth might unfold over time, consider the sequence of activities employed by a hypothetical nonprofit I'll call The Hospital.

PHASE 1: THE WELCOME CYCLE

The Hospital's high-dollar donor acquisition effort, and the activities that ensue once the first gift is received, proceed in a series of five steps:

1 Early in the spring, The Hospital's development staff mails invitations to one thousand of its most generous and responsive donors to enroll in The Advocates.

This newly-minted giving society requires an annual contribution of at least $1,000. The funds will underwrite health education in the community designed to lower the markedly high rates of diabetes, heart disease, and stroke that are prevalent there.

Forty-seven of the invitees respond to the mailing with gifts. Twenty-three send checks for $1,000 or more.

2 Immediately upon receiving each gift, the person opening the mail calls the donor to acknowledge the gift and express delight. (Research indicates that it's the speed of the thank-you that's critical, not who does the thanking.)

3 Within 24 hours of receiving each gift, Hospital staff mails a personalized thank-you letter to the donor. Those who have chosen to enlist in The Advocates are warmly welcomed into the fold and informed that their gifts will be put to work immediately to fund The

71

Hospital's health education work.

Their letters are produced on special Advocates letterhead and mailed in matching envelopes. Others are told in letters using standard Hospital stationery that their gifts will assist Hospital staff in providing urgently needed care to the community's most needy residents.

In every letter, the amount and date of the contribution is cited. Every letter is personally signed by the Vice President, Development, who adds a brief, handwritten postscript on the bottom of the page adding his personal thanks.

4 Later that same week the Vice President, Development mails a second, personalized letter to newly enrolled Advocates.

He introduces Advocates to their Personal Liaison in the development department, an individual designated by name, direct telephone number, and email address. Any Advocate may turn to this person with questions, concerns, or suggestions for the community health education program.

The Vice President's letter also paints a broad picture of The Hospital's development program, explaining to Advocates what other philanthropic opportunities exist at The Hospital, including other giving societies, the annual gala dinner, the celebrity golf tournament, and legacy giving. Gently, he invites recipients to consider whether any friends, family members, or colleagues might be candidates for some role as donors.

Along with the letter is a brief, personalized questionnaire – not an anonymous survey – that solicits information about each donor's communication and solicitation preferences; views about healthcare; demographic and lifestyle characteristics; and potential interest in legacy giving.

The questionnaire also includes space for donors to write in names and addresses of potential new donors and a blank space encouraging comments. A pre-addressed reply envelope bearing a first-class stamp is included in the package.

5 Ten days later, every one of the 23 new members of The Advocates receives an informative, three-page letter from the physician in charge of The Hospital's community health education program.

This letter details the community's principal health challenges, citing a few (but not many!) statistics. The physician expresses warm appreciation on her behalf and that of her staff. She closes with an invitation to phone a specific number at the hospital to inquire about the calendar of health education sessions.

•••

Compare that sequence of activities to the typical treatment fundraisers mete out to direct mail donors. Think about the thoughtfulness, the appreciation, the genuine concern those communications convey.

You'll probably think about the cost, too – cost in terms of both time and money. But, as the process continues to unfold, you'll discover what a huge return your organization will receive for investing in donor-centered fundraising.

PHASE 2: RESOLICITATION BEGINS

In a high-dollar fundraising program, asking for additional gifts becomes an integral element in an ongoing program of donor cultivation, education, and involvement. But every communication, whether a request for money or an update on The Hospital's work, also brims over with appreciation.

6 Three weeks after the letter from the director of the community health education program, the members of The Advocates receive a one-page bulletin – a miniature newsletter, really – that is specifically designed to report to them on The Hospital's work in health education.

Unlike other materials produced by The Hospital's marketing department, this mini-newsletter is printed in black on white recycled paper and appears to be coming straight from a laser-printer right on the program director's desk. (This is not far off the mark. However, the laser-printer resides in the development department).

The headline story in the bulletin announces the first of what are foreseen as occasional conference-call briefings on new developments in the program. This first call, one hour long, will feature the program's director and a diabetes specialist discussing a recent breakthrough in diabetes prevention work.

7 The following week, six of The Advocates call into a regional toll-free number for the one-hour briefing on new approaches to diabetes prevention. The discussion is lively, with four of the six Advocates asking multiple questions of the medical staffers.

8 Three months later, following a second issue of the bulletin, the 16 Advocates who have not insisted on being solicited once per year receive a special appeal. This high-dollar package, produced with the same high production values, hand labor, and attention to detail, requests special gifts of $1,000, $2,000, or more to help match a foundation challenge grant to fund an innovative pilot project to establish blood pressure checkpoints in grocery stores, pharmacies, and churches.

9 Four of the 16 Advocates included in the special appeal respond with contributions. The average gift is nearly $4,000, because one of the four sends $10,000 and another sends $2,000.

10 The Vice President, Development, personally phones every one of the four special appeal donors to thank them for their generosity.

PHASE 3: THE YEAR-END CYCLE

It is said that 40 percent of all individual gifts are made during the final quarter of the calendar year (at least in North America). Any American fundraiser would be a fool to overlook that cultural and psychological reality and the tax-deductibility of gifts that so many high-dollar donors take so seriously.

That's why The Hospital takes pains to intensify its communication program during the last three months of the year.

11 Early in the autumn The Advocates receive a third issue of the bulletin. A cover letter offers them complimentary $250 tickets to The Hospital's annual gala dinner. All they need do is call or email their Personal Liaison to make the arrangements.

12 Late in the autumn, at The Hospital's annual gala dinner, the nine Advocates who have accepted complimentary tickets are seated at a special table along with the director of the community health education program and their Personal Liaison in the development office. Except for those who wish to remain anonymous, they are also recognized from the podium.

13 At year-end, all 23 Advocates—now joined by an additional 19 donors who responded to a more recent invitation to the program – receive end-of-year high-dollar appeals. (For seven of the 23, this is their first solicitation since becoming Advocates. For the other 16, it is their second.) Recipients (except for those who have already given $2,000 or more) are asked to consider enrolling at the $2,000 level in The Advocates program.

The $2,000 special-appeal donor is asked whether he wishes to join at the $5,000 level by contributing an additional $3,000.

The $10,000 donor is thanked profusely once again and informed that he has been admitted as a Charter Member at the $10,000 level and will receive a special invitation to join the health education director and the Vice President, Development at an intimate dinner in the near future.

14 Six of the 23 original Advocates respond generously to the year-end appeal. Their gifts are quickly, warmly, and appropriately acknowledged with a mixture of letters and phone calls (as specified in the information they supplied in response to the initial questionnaire). They are all informed they will be considered members in good standing of The Advocates throughout the new year.

PHASE 4: THE RENEWAL CYCLE

Many direct mail practitioners insist that a membership program, or anything that smells like one, is a sure-fire formula to lower the average number of gifts per donor per year. They may be right. But they ignore at their peril the potential for such a program to produce much higher renewal rates and increased donor loyalty.

An annual cycle that includes a specific request for renewed support (whether dues or contributions) helps engender in donors *the habit of giving*. A higher renewal rate and a longer donor lifetime more than offset a lower number of gifts per donor.

That's why I feel so strongly that such an approach is ideally suited for a high-dollar program, and even more particularly so for one that's based on a giving club such as The Advocates. The Hospital has adopted this approach.

15 Early in the new year, the 17 original Advocates who did not respond to the end-of-year solicitation receive the first letter in a four-effort renewal series. This is a high-dollar letter similar to others, except that it's much briefer and to-the-point. It asks Advocates to renew their support for the new calendar year by matching the amounts they sent the previous year – or, if possible, by stepping up to a higher level in the program.

16 The four Advocates who respond to the first renewal notice are immediately acknowledged, as usual.

17 The other 13 Advocates fall into two categories: four who have specified they wish to be solicited only once annually, and nine who have not. Three weeks after the first renewal notice is mailed, the four annual-only donors are either phoned or sent personal notes from the Vice President, Development to remind them that they had requested once-a-year fund appeals but haven't yet responded.

Another two weeks later, staff mails the second renewal notice to the other nine Advocates. Later still, at one-month intervals, third and fourth renewal notices are sent to those donors who have neglected to respond to the first two notices.

•••

And so it goes. The cycle repeats.

For those donors who enroll in a high-dollar giving society such as The Advocates but do not renew in the following year, it's probably best to continue treating them as members of the society for a second year. Only following two years of non-response would it make sense to return them to the standard appeal and renewal stream.

But it's worth making one more try to recapture the passion that led them to enlist in the society, either through a personalized mailing that includes a brief questionnaire seeking the reason for the lapse in giving, or through a phone call with a similar objective.

As in any annual donor renewal program, the rewards are cumulative. As the process unfolds over time, the number of high-dollar donors grows each year, and their renewal rates tend to rise as the membership of the giving society consists of an ever-larger proportion of multi-year donors whose renewals may be essentially reflexive. Upgrades tend to raise the average gift as well. The upshot is a continuing increase in net revenue from the program.

There is an even bigger picture, however. In fundraising generally, but most especially in high-dollar fundraising, it's essential to consider the long haul. That's the topic I'll take up in the following chapter, "Sustaining your returns over the long haul."

Sustaining Your Returns Over the Long Haul

When you venture outside the realm of traditional direct mail fundraising, you'll encounter a variety of fundraising programs and techniques that may mystify you if your background is largely in direct marketing.

Programs in major gifts, legacy giving, and one or more capital campaigns may co-exist at a thriving nonprofit organization or institution. These programs represent the top of the fundraising pyramid and often account for 80% or more of an organization's philanthropic income.

It's therefore no shame to think of the work you're doing in high-dollar direct mail as a path for donors to follow toward such programs. After all, at many nonprofits, a single major gift or legacy could equal all the revenue you realize in years of direct mail fundraising.

Cultivating likely prospects for such gifts is justification enough to invest in high-dollar direct mail. But regardless of whether your objective is current revenue from a high-dollar program itself or future revenue in the form of truly large gifts, you won't get very far unless you set yourself up for a long-haul effort.

Four ideas form the basis of a successful long-term high-dollar fundraising program:

1) The annual giving society
2) An annual renewal process
3) A high-dollar newsletter (or the equivalent)
4) A year-round annual communications schedule

Let's look at those ideas, one at a time.

1) The annual giving society

A high-dollar annual giving society or club isn't essential, but it helps a lot. As fundraisers have learned at universities, hospitals, and cultural institutions, the annual giving society provides a convenient mechanism to offer donor benefits in a structured way.

Having structured levels of giving also helps persuade donors to upgrade by leaps and bounds rather than in incremental steps. The same is true in any nonprofit that's prepared to launch a high-dollar direct mail fundraising program.

One of the essential ingredients in any giving society is a snazzy name that suits the character of the organization and reflects the appropriate degree of prestige that attaches to high-dollar giving. For example, a $1,000-a-year giving club at The Nature Conservancy is called the Rachel Carson Society, borrowing the name of one of the environmental movement's patron saints.

At colleges and universities the high-dollar society often bears a name such as The President's Council or the Chancellor's Circle to signal the high-level access that such generous donors receive.

Many institutions expand the concept of the high-dollar giving society into a tier of clubs at ever-increasing levels with ever-expanding benefits. For example, to return to the hypothetical Hospital we visited in the last chapter, The Advocates might be offered opportunities to upgrade to the Silver, Gold, Platinum, and Diamond levels by giving $2,500, $5,000, $10,000, or $25,000 per year.

Alternatively, each of these levels could be viewed as a separate giving society with its own distinctive name. At an even larger institution, donors could be invited to join exclusive giving circles at the level of $100,000 or even $1,000,000 per year.

Naturally, the more levels or giving societies you organize, the more trouble you'll have keeping track of the distinctions among the benefits they merit. In fact, you may have trouble coming up with enough benefits in the first place. (That's a common problem.)

High-dollar benefits vary hugely from one nonprofit to another, but they tend to fall into one or more of five categories:

• Access to powerful, influential, or famous people, or merely to the beneficiaries of their giving;

• Opportunities for tours, site visits, or even overseas travel to view the organization's work up close;

• Distinct levels of public recognition;

• Physical tokens of membership such as commemorative plaques, autographed copies of books, lapel pins or other jewelry; and

• Membership privileges such as free admission to events or designated parking spots.

There's no limit to what the imagination can dredge up – and that's why it's so important to keep uppermost in mind that *many high-dollar donors couldn't care less about such benefits.*

What they care about is how their gifts help you achieve your mission. And what they tend to appreciate most is that you acknowledge their participation in your work and give them frequent opportunities to learn how you're putting their gifts to work. (This doesn't mean you shouldn't bother to offer tangible benefits. After all, some donors regard such benefits as a big incentive to give generously. But I recommend that high-dollar donors be offered the option to *decline* tangible benefits.)

Many nonprofits construct a tier of giving societies, usually beginning at the nice round number of $1,000 per year. Some also establish lower-level clubs (at the $250 and $500 levels, for example) as a way to move direct mail-acquired donors more gradually up the ladder. At whatever level, a giving society is most valuable in encouraging donors to make regular, annual contributions. That requires establishing an annual renewal process.

2) An annual renewal process

The human race has developed innumerable ways to cut and slice time. We can measure its passage in milliseconds or millennia. But there are only three units of time that resonate in our bones: the day, because the sun marks its coming and going; the month, because the cycle of the moon still governs our lives in so many ways; and the year. We measure our lives in years.

On a much more prosaic level, most donors tend to think about their support for nonprofit causes and institutions on an *annual basis*. That's why the annual fund, the annual campaign, and annual membership programs have loomed so large in the nonprofit sector.

High-dollar donors act in much the same way as any others. The annual giving society reflects that reality, and the annual renewal cycle makes it work.

Any annual renewal program is based on three assumptions about donor behavior:

A) A regular annual contribution gives a donor or member a sense of continuing participation in work she values highly. This reinforces the satisfaction she feels for providing her ongoing support.

B) Donors who are committed to a cause or institution – especially those who have supported it for many years – often need little more than a gentle reminder to send their annual gifts. In other words, it's rarely necessary to provide donors with an elaborate rationale for renewing their support.

C) Few donors pay close attention to the communications they receive from the organizations they support. It might take three, four, or more letters before it penetrates a donor's consciousness that she hasn't mailed her contribution for the year.

The annual renewal series – modeled on the subscription renewal series developed many decades ago by magazine publishers – is designed on the basis of these three premises. The fundraiser mails a sequence of (generally short) letters to each donor, removing a donor from mailings of subsequent letters once she has made a gift.

In a traditional, small-dollar direct mail fundraising program, a renewal series might consist of as many as 10 notices or "efforts." Rarely would I consider more than half that number in a high-dollar program, partly because the numbers are usually too small to justify the expenditure, and partly because most high-dollar donors require kid-glove treatment that won't permit such a persistent (and potentially irritating) series of communications.

The annual renewal series seeks to persuade each member of a high-dollar giving society to contribute at least once each year. If the series is well crafted, most high-dollar donors will comply. Some of them, but a minority, may contribute to an occasional special appeal or year-end campaign as well. But, over time, the renewal series for a high-dollar society is likely to generate the lion's share of revenue in the program.

3) A high-dollar newsletter (or the equivalent)

Successful direct mail fundraising requires that donors regularly receive information about the work of the charities and institutions they support. Repeated appeals for funds aren't enough, even if you rationalize that they provide a lot of information.

The overwhelming majority of direct mail fundraisers defy this all-too-obvious lesson, even though donor research and (more to the point) declining rates of response and fast-falling renewal rates confirm its importance.

Donors crave information. There is a direct correlation between donor loyalty and the frequency with which donors receive information about how their gifts are used. Longitudinal testing in direct mail programs confirms that donor newsletters substantially enhance donor loyalty. This lesson is triply important in a high-dollar program, which is built on the understanding that donor involvement, cultivation, and education are central to the fundraising process.

There are many ways development staff members, volunteers, or board members can help nurture relationships with high-dollar donors. Here are just a few:

• Distribute a periodic personalized letter from the chief executive reporting on new developments and new insights about the organization's work.

• Make occasional phone calls, not necessarily to thank donors for recent contributions but merely to stay in touch.

• Send copies of important internal memos, reports, or proposals from time to time.

• Organize briefings or telephone conference calls to give donors opportunities to ask questions directly of key staff members.

• Mail personal notes to mark birthdays or holidays.

• Send clippings from newspapers or magazines either directly about the organization's work or about an issue that's central to its mission.

• Invite high-dollar donors as guests to special events.

• Send such tokens of appreciation as an autographed book written by a staff or board member, or an elegant item bearing the organization's logo.

Used frequently enough, techniques of this sort can eliminate the need for a high-dollar newsletter. However, if your organization is like most nonprofits, with trustees' and staff members' time at a premium, it's unlikely that such activities will take place year-round. To ensure continuous communication, you should consider producing a high-dollar newsletter.

A high-dollar newsletter need not resemble a run-of-the-mill direct mail donor newsletter in any significant way. You don't have to mail the newsletter on a rigid, three-, four-, or six-times-per-year schedule.

In fact, in my opinion, it's better for a high-dollar newsletter to have the look and feel of an occasional bulletin pulled together when something of significance comes to light and then rushed into the mail. I don't even think it's necessary to include photographs, which seem indispensable for most donor newsletters.

For example, a high-dollar newsletter might be devoted to any of the following items:

• A report from the field when the chief executive or a key program staff member returns to the office

• An update from an important and revealing meeting of the board of trustees

• A thoughtful letter from the chief executive or other top staff person reflecting on the larger meaning of the group's work

• An analysis of the organization's long-term impact

Any material that helps convey to high-dollar donors that they're receiving inside information is fair game for a high-dollar newsletter.

4) A year-round annual communications schedule

In chapter 6, I sketched out the sequence of actions employed by The Hospital. The mailings, phone calls, and other activities described a well-considered plan of approach reflecting years of experience in high-dollar direct mail fundraising.

First, as you'll recall, there was a cycle of activity revolving around the recruitment and orientation of new giving society members. That cycle included an invitation or acquisition package; two formal thank-you letters; a questionnaire soliciting new members' views and preferences; and an introduction to the newsletter developed exclusively for members of the giving society. Such a cycle may begin at any time of the year when new members are enrolled. At some point, however, those new members will be folded into an ongoing high-dollar communications program.

An ongoing program comprises four types of activity – solicitation, involvement, education, and cultivation – which are reflected in the table on the facing page.

I hope you won't slavishly follow this calendar of activities. I'm presenting it as an approach that combines year-round solicitation with involvement, education, and cultivation, all with a view toward the long haul. With proper consideration for individual donors' preferences and quirks, a varied combination of communications such as this will sustain their loyalty and generosity for many years to come.

Why? Why does it work? Let's consider that in this book's final chapter.

Model High-Dollar Fundraising Program

MONTH	SOLICIT	INVOLVE	EDUCATE	CULTIVATE
January			Cultivation mailing #1	
February	Renewal mailing #1 with annual Donor Preference Survey			
March	Renewal mailing #2		High-dollar newsletter #1	
April	Renewal mailing #3			Reception with leadership
May	Renewal mailing #4 with spring mail appeal	———— Conference call briefing #1 ————		
June	Renewal phone call		Cultivation mailing #2	
July		Donor consultation group*	High-dollar newsletter #2	
August			Cultivation mailing #3	
September		———— Conference call briefing #2 ————		
October			High-dollar newsletter #3	Comp. seats at gala dinner
November	Year-end mailing			
December	Follow-up to year-end mailing by mail or phone			

* *An informal focus group*

So, Why Does This Stuff Work?

When I speak at fundraising conferences and workshops, I some-times ask those in attendance to raise their hands if they personally give to "charity."

Often I then ask if they respond to direct mail fundraising appeals. If the audience is on the younger side, it's not unusual that a bare majority raise their hands in response to the first question – and a much smaller number to the second.

The lesson of this experience is obvious: many fundraisers, espe-cially younger ones, aren't donors themselves. At least they're not the *habitual* donors who populate direct mail donor lists.

Is it any wonder, then, that so many fundraisers lack appreciation of the dynamics of direct mail?

Now, don't get me wrong. Direct mail donors – at any level – don't usually understand their own giving behavior, either. For example, in focus groups and interviews, donors consistently underestimate the number of nonprofit causes and institutions they support. They fail to recall how frequently they give. Sometimes they don't even remember which nonprofits they contribute to.

I wish I could tell you that, unlike most of the rest of humanity, *I* understand why direct mail donors appear so unobservant about their charitable giving – much less why they're so generous.

In fact, though I've personally contributed by mail for many years and have myself become a high-dollar donor, and though I've conducted high-dollar direct mail fundraising campaigns for a quarter-century, I won't pretend to know exactly why direct mail in general, and high-dollar direct mail in particular, is so successful.

Reliable research findings are hard to come by, and the research my colleagues and I have conducted is in the form of "testing." Direct mail tests, properly conducted, are rigorous and scientific in a broad sense of the term, but they only tell us *what* works, not *why*.

I don't mean we're clueless about why donors choose to give. Attitudinal research into donor motivation is plentiful. I delved into that topic in chapter 3, so you know I believe donors are just as likely to be motivated by positive emotions such as hope, love, faith, duty, and compassion as they are by the negative ones that most marketers (and too many fundraisers) emphasize.

But this understanding begs the question of why *direct mail* works. High-dollar donors may contribute to the causes and institutions they favor in face-to-face encounters, at special events, by telephone, online, or in other, more imaginative ways. Many do. But why does high-dollar mail figure into the picture? Why do these same people respond with large gifts to a mailing?

I'm going to give you a straight answer now. But don't shoot me.

The regrettable truth is, I can only *guess* why high-dollar mail has been so successful for me and my colleagues. Here are some of the conclusions I've drawn after years of thinking about this question:

- High-dollar direct mail fundraising works *when you pick the right list.* As every direct marketing practitioner knows to a fault, targeting is the biggest challenge in the field – and the most important.

Other factors pale beside it. In high-dollar direct mail, you've got to mail to people who have enough money available to respond at the levels you're asking for.

• High-dollar direct mail fundraising works *when you craft – and convincingly communicate – an appropriate and compelling case for giving.*

If you're appealing to well-educated people with a sophisticated grasp of the issues and challenges your organization confronts, and if you respond in kind with messaging that doesn't insult their intelligence, you're clearly on the right track.

• High-dollar direct mail fundraising works *when you package your appeals in ways that suggest real people wrote and mailed them.*

At direct mail seminars and workshops, the question at the top of the agenda often is "How do you break through the clutter?" High-dollar direct mail breaks through with high production values, a look of importance, and a human touch. It's persuasively personal in ways that direct mail normally isn't.

Still, when all is said and done, the fundamental reason why high-dollar direct mail fundraising will work for *you* is that it will require you to treat your best donors the way they want to be treated.

As many wiser souls than I have repeatedly said, fundraising is an art. Particularly in direct response, there are scientific aspects of our work that help bolster our confidence that we're doing things right. But, at its heart, fundraising is what the late Hank Rosso called a "gentle art."

And the best high-dollar direct mail fundraising, evoking and simulating the intimacy of face-to-face fundraising, is an expression of that gentle art. Clearly, it's not the market-driven, transactional approach that has dominated direct mail fundraising since it evolved in its contemporary form more than half a century ago.

If in a sensitive and artful way you use the techniques described in this book, you'll touch your donors' hearts – and the many gifts you'll receive in their lifetimes of giving will justify all the investment you make in money, effort, and time.

Equally important, you'll find partners who share your passion for the cause, whatever that may be. Their compassion will sustain you in your work, touch your heart, and enrich your life.

Whoever thought direct mail could do that?

APPENDIX

Will high-dollar mail work in politics, too?

You bet. In fact, over the years my colleagues and I have had remarkable success in the mail, raising gifts of $1,000 or more for political candidates and committees. Much of the money we generated for the Presidential campaigns of Senator Gary Hart, Rev. Jesse Jackson, and four other Democratic Presidential candidates came in this form.

The sample appeal from Wellstone Action! that's depicted in these pages lies squarely in this tradition. The organization was founded early in 2003 by David and Mark Wellstone, sons of the late Senator Paul Wellstone (D-MN).

In October 2002, just weeks before election day, the Senator, his wife Sheila, their daughter, two campaign aides, and two pilots lost their lives in a tragic airplane crash in rural Minnesota.

Paul Wellstone was regarded by many liberal and progressive activists as the most principled and articulate voice who championed the rights of working families in America. Together, he and his wife Sheila were among the country's most beloved political leaders, with supporters not just on the left of the spectrum but on the right as well.

Mark and David, along with a number of the Wellstones' loyal campaign staff and volunteers, launched Wellstone Action! to carry on Paul and Sheila's legacy. Since then, Wellstone Action! has been training thousands of people around the country in Paul Wellstone's unique brand of successful political organizing; mobilizing the huge national base of Wellstone donors and volunteers into a compelling force for change; and extending Sheila Wellstone's behind-the-scenes role coordinating national efforts to combat domestic violence.

The appeal reproduced here was mailed two years after the death of Paul and Sheila Wellstone. It represents a successful effort to launch the new Wellstone Action! Organizers Circle, a $1,000-per-year giving society. This package utilizes a "proposal" format, one of a number of effective approaches to high-dollar packaging.

Appendix: 1.0 - Wellstone Action! • Actual Size: 9" x 12"

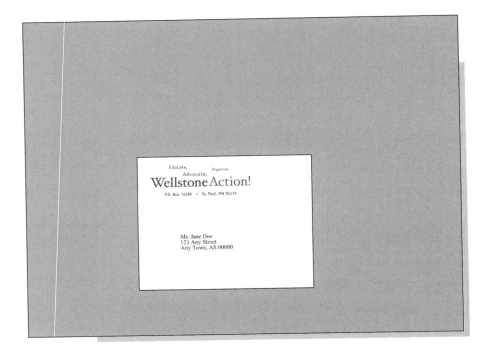

Educate.

Organize.

Advocate.

Wellstone Action!

P.O. Box 14386 • St. Paul, MN 55114

Organizer's Circle

St. Paul, Minnesota
October 20, 2004

Ms. Jane Doe
123 Any Street
Any Town, AS 00000

Dear Ms. Doe,

In a few weeks, Americans will go to the polls in one of the most important elections in our history.

The stakes have never been higher, and it's almost certain that the outcome will once again be decided by a narrow margin—with the edge going to the side that does a better job of finding supporters and getting them to the polls.

As one of the most generous contributors to my Dad's Senate campaigns, I know you share my hope—and my fears—about the outcome of this election.

But whatever the results on November 2, our real work begins the very next day. That's because we're not fixated on winning a single election. Rather, here at Wellstone Action, **our goal is to advance the progressive agenda in communities and states across the country, now and in the future.**

I'm pleased to report that we've already made tremendous progress. As you'll see below, we've redoubled our efforts to train activists to ensure we get out the vote this November. And we've conducted special Camp Wellstones in key battleground states such as Florida, Washington, and Ohio.

Since our founding in 2003, we've trained over 5,000 individuals at 35 camps in 25 states. We're proud of the work we are doing. We believe it's making a lasting contribution to building a new progressive movement in this country.

But to move forward, we need the sustained commitment of everyone who agrees with the ideals and vision embodied in my parents' work.

That's why I'm inviting you to join the Wellstone Action Organizer's Circle with a gift of $1,000 or more today.

As a member of the Organizer's Circle, you'll play a leadership role in securing a progressive future for America—whatever the outcome of the November 2 election.

I've enclosed a proposal that outlines our goals for the year ahead. With your help, we

Appendix: 1.2 - Wellstone Action!

can meet our goals of training 2,000 more activists in 2005—and grow the Wellstone Action Network to reach a total of 100,000 activists countrywide next year.

And you'll be helping us build on the important work we've been doing during the run-up to this year's elections:

- **Camp Wellstone.** We're holding four major trainings this fall in Seattle, Cleveland, Denver, and San Francisco to bolster our efforts to get out the vote on November 2. These intensive two-day training sessions focus heavily on the final push to get out the vote (GOTV), covering the elements of an effective, energetic, and winning GOTV effort.

- **The Green Bus Tour.** In mid-September, the Wellstone Green Bus took the show on the road across Minnesota to bring more training and action in grassroots politics to the people. This enduring symbol of Paul Wellstone and the power of grassroots activism traveled to five cities providing training in organizing and hands-on practice to progressive organizers across the state.

- **Organizing Online.** With more than 50,000 members, Wellstone Action is a phenomenon that keeps on growing. Not everyone can attend Camp Wellstone, so we've put the skills we teach online.

Wellstone Action, like my parents, finds its strength in the work and commitment of tens of thousands of volunteer activists working on the ground. But the spark that gives momentum to this grassroots movement comes from people like you.

At this pivotal moment, when we'll find out whether the interests of ordinary people working together can triumph over special interests and moneyed politics, the leadership of a few good people like you can make all the difference.

That's why I urge you to join the Organizer's Circle today with a gift of $1,000 or more.

If a gift in that amount isn't possible for you right now, my brother and I will be grateful for any contribution you can send. But please act now, so we can continue the momentum we've gained this year into the years to come.

Together, we can keep the progressive agenda alive by rebuilding a movement, one person at a time, through training, networking, and organizing. Together, we will prevail, ensuring that this great nation shall serve the needs of working families, not corporate profiteers.

With great hope,

David Wellstone

P.S. If you join the Wellstone Action Organizer's Circle with a gift of $1,000 or more, I'll be pleased to send you a copy of my Dad's book, *The Conscience of a Liberal*. You will also receive our newsletter, along with special updates. Thank you!

Wellstone Action Strategy
2005 Proposal

Prepared for:

Jane Doe

"The people of this country, not special interest big money, should be the source of all political power."

—Paul Wellstone 1944-2002

Educate.   Organize.
Advocate.
Wellstone Action!

P.O. Box 14386 • St. Paul, MN 55114

MISSION

"Politics isn't about big money or power games; it's about the improvement of people's lives."

—Paul Wellstone (1944-2002)

Throughout his life Paul Wellstone worked tirelessly for progressive change and economic justice. Though he was often a lone voice during his two terms in Washington, since his tragic death thousands of people have taken up his mission to work for progressive ideals and change.

Wellstone Action galvanizes this groundswell of support for the progressive agenda. Using the Wellstone Action website, email action alerts, grassroots organizing, and partnerships with like-minded organizations, the advocacy network puts its weight and energy behind a series of issues—working on and winning one campaign at a time.

In the current political climate, Wellstone Action's work is more urgent than ever. Faced with entrenched special interests and deep-pocketed corporate influence, Wellstone Action is training and organizing a large national network of committed individuals united by progressive values.

Wellstone Action is capitalizing on these huge assets to continue the fight for a better, more just and sustainable future for all Americans.

2005 PROGRAM GOALS

Camp Wellstone: Train 2,000 New Activists at 13 Camps in 10 States $260,000

Camp Wellstone is a highly acclaimed, hands-on, three-day training program for anyone who has an interest in running for elected office, working on a political campaign, or simply becoming an effective citizen or activist or leader. It focuses on the nuts and bolts of working on progressive issues and successfully electing progressive candidates. The workshop introduces participants to Paul Wellstone's distinctive approach to politics—combining the power of grassroots organizing with citizen participation to defeat the power of big money.

Appendix: 1.5 - Wellstone Action!

Wellstone Action is committed to providing these training sessions to anyone who is interested, regardless of financial means. While the cost of training an individual is approximately $200, we keep the actual cost to participants low. For three days of training, participants pay just $50 ($35 for students and lower income individuals), which barely covers the cost of their food and materials.

Since Wellstone Action's founding in 2003, Camp Wellstone has experienced high demand, with sessions often filling up within 24 hours. One reporter who participated in the Camp said, "The camps are practical and tactical. They seek to implement the call to arms Wellstone sounded in his 2001 book *The Conscience of a Liberal*: 'In every state, we need to get serious about developing leaders—starting with school board, city council, county commissioner, mayoral, and state legislative races.'"

Wellstone Action Network:
Grow to 100,000 Active Members $30,000

The Wellstone Action Network is a growing grassroots political force connected through email, our website, and "meet-ups." Through direct advocacy campaigns and partnerships with like-minded organizations, the Network concentrates on major issues championed by Paul and Sheila Wellstone.

The Network's first action was mobilizing support for the Paul Wellstone Mental Health Equitable Treatment Act. This legislation requires that mental illness be treated the same as physical illness. Network activists wrote thousands of emails and letters and made thousands of phone calls. Using our web-based instant action feature, people around the country sent 24,000 faxes to key legislators in Congress.

During 2005, with the help of new technology and our online organizer, we will grow the Wellstone Action Network to 100,000 members, and work on one or two significant, winnable progressive issue campaigns.

The Sheila Wellstone Institute:
Continue the Work to Prevent Domestic Violence $84,000

Wellstone Action is proud to continue Sheila Wellstone's effective work in bringing public attention to the problem of domestic violence and insisting that it be on the political agenda of our country. The Sheila Wellstone Institute is launching an initiative—Camp Sheila Wellstone—designed to embolden efforts to make ending domestic violence and sexual assault a civic and political priority. Efforts to end domestic violence and sexual assault can be magnified by the power of grassroots organizing. This initiative will bring training and tools to advocates and practitioners, organizational staff and board members, and dedicated community members committed to stopping violence against women and children and helping those hurt by violence. The first of these Camp Sheila Wellstone trainings was held in Minnesota this spring. We plan to hold seven Camps across the U.S. in 2005. Each Camp costs $12,000 to produce.

THE NEED

The Wellstone Approach to political action and social justice can have a profound and positive impact on the political landscape of this country. Americans have shown they are ready for this type of hands-on politics. Over five thousand have enthusiastically taken the Camp Wellstone activist training, and tens of thousands have joined the Wellstone Action Network.

Now, Wellstone Action needs the resources to reach out to thousands more Americans who are ready and willing to become active. Wellstone Action's first-year success was funded, in large part, by the most committed contributors to Paul Wellstone's 2002 Senate campaign. To build on its initial success, the Wellstone Action Network needs more committed contributors to step forward with funding. This leadership is fundamental to the long-term vision of Paul and Sheila Wellstone.

Wellstone Action Advisory Committee

This impressive group of individuals has been assembled to provide guidance and leadership for Wellstone Action's work.

Marcia Avner	Frances Fox Piven	Brigid McDonough	R.T. Rybak
Warren Beatty	Al Franken	Jerry McEntee	Andy Stern
Julian Bond	Leo Gerard	Colin McGinnis	Sarah Stoesz
Heather Booth	Tom Harkin	Alida Messinger	Antonio Villaraigosa
Bob Borosage	Jim Hightower	Howard Metzenbaum	David Wellstone –
Bill Bradley	Arthur Himmelman	Kari Moe	Co-Chair
Donna Brazile	Sam Kaplan	Walter Mondale	Mark Wellstone –
Mark Dayton	Sylvia Kaplan	Mee Moua	Co-Chair
Ron DeHarpporte	Jonathan Kozol	Tom O'Connell	Peter Yarrow
Peter Edelman	Susan Lenfestey	Robert Redford	
Russ Feingold	John Lewis	Robert Reich	
David Foster	Juan Linares	Mark Ritchie	

"I don't represent the big oil companies, I don't represent the big pharmaceutical companies, I don't represent the Enrons of this world, but you know what, they already have great representation in Washington. It's the rest of the people that need it. I represent the people of Minnesota."

—Paul Wellstone

WAC4-AF5

MEMORANDUM OF ACCEPTANCE

2005 Wellstone Action Organizer's Circle

Ms. Jane Doe
123 Any Street
Any Town, AS 00000

04AFDOE-E   0

I share your determination that this great nation shall serve the needs of working families, not corporate profiteers. And I understand that achieving this goal will require disciplined and steady work for many years—regardless of the outcome of the November 2 election.

That's why I want to take a leadership role in helping Wellstone Action build on its strong and successful start.

[ ] Please enroll me as a member of the Wellstone Action Organizer's Circle, and keep me updated about this year's progress. My first annual gift of $1,000 or more is enclosed.

[ ] $1,000   [ ] $1,500

[ ] Please send my complimentary copy of Paul Wellstone's book, *The Conscience of a Liberal.*

[ ] I am not able to become a member of the Organizer's Circle at this time, but I'm joining Wellstone Action. I'm enclosing my first year's contribution of $_____.

☐ My check is enclosed.
☐ Please bill my: ☐ Visa ☐ MasterCard   Number _____

Exp. date _____   Signature (for credit cards only) _____

Please sign me up for regular Wellstone Action network email updates. My email address is:

_____.

Wellstone Action is a nonprofit organization under Section 501(c)(4) of the U.S Internal Revenue Code. Contributions support Wellstone Action's grassroots organizing, lobbying and campaigns and are thus not tax-deductible.

The Wellstone Action Fund is a separate 501(c)(3) nonprofit organization formed exclusively to fund the charitable and educational functions of Wellstone Action. Gifts to the Wellstone Action Fund are tax-deductible as provided by law.

Please return this form with your contribution in the enclosed postage-paid envelope, or mail to David Wellstone, Wellstone Action, P.O. Box 14386, St. Paul, MN 55114. Thank you very much for caring!

Educate.   Organize.
Advocate.
Wellstone Action!

P.O. Box 14386 • St. Paul, MN 55114 .

RECYCLED & RECYCLABLE / SOY INK   WAC4-AF2

Appendix: 1.8 - Wellstone Action! • Actual size: 8-7/8" x 3-7/8"

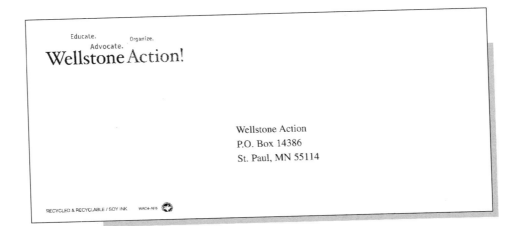

ABOUT THE AUTHOR

Consultant, author, and public speaker Mal Warwick has been involved in the not-for-profit sector for more than 40 years.

• Mal is the founder and chairman of Mal Warwick & Associates, Inc. (Berkeley, Calif.), a fundraising and marketing agency that has served nonprofit organizations since 1979, and of its sister company, Response Management Technologies, Inc., a data processing firm for nonprofit organizations. He is also co-founder (with Nick Allen) of Donordigital (San Francisco, Calif., and Washington, DC), which assists nonprofit organizations online, and was a co-founder of Share Group, Inc. (Somerville, Mass.), one of the nation's leading telephone fundraising firms.

• This is Mal's 17th book. His previous works include the standard texts, *Revolution in the Mailbox* and *How to Write Successful Fundraising Letters,* both of which are now in second editions.

• He is editor of *Mal Warwick's Newsletter: Successful Direct Mail, Telephone & Online Fundraising*™, and is a popular speaker and workshop leader throughout the world. He has taught fundraising on six continents to nonprofit executives from more than 100 countries.

Among the hundreds of nonprofits Mal and his colleagues have served over the years are many of the nation's largest and most distinguished charities as well as six Democratic Presidential candidates and scores of small, local, and regional organizations. Collectively, Mal and his associates are responsible for raising at least half a billion dollars—largely in the form of small gifts from individuals.

Mal is an active member of the Association of Fundraising Professionals (Alexandria, VA); a member of the Board of the Resource Alliance (London, UK), organizers of the annual International Fundraising Congress in Amsterdam, and the Congress' Ambassador to the USA; and served for ten years on the board of the Association of Direct Response Fundraising Counsel (Washington, D.C.), two of those years as President. In 2004, he received the Hank Rosso Award as Outstanding Fundraising Executive from the Association of Fundraising Professionals Golden Gate Chapter and Northern California Grantmakers.

Since 1990, Mal has been active in promoting social and environmental responsibility in the nationwide business community. He was a co-founder of Business for Social Responsibility in 1992 and served on its board during its inaugural year. In 2001, he was elected to the board of the Social Venture Network and now serves as Chair.

Mal was a Peace Corps Volunteer in Ecuador for more than three years. Since 1969 he has lived in Berkeley, California, where he is deeply involved in local community affairs. Early in the 1990s, he co-founded the Community Bank of the Bay, the nation's fifth community development bank, and the Berkeley Community Fund, where he remains active on the board. He also served for 11 years as Vice-President of the Board of the Berkeley Symphony (1991-2002).

He is the grandfather of Dayna, Iain, Matthew, Gwen, Andrew, Kaili, and Benjamin, who live with their various parents or on college campuses throughout the United States.

FOR ADDITIONAL READING

For insight into the values and feelings that help explain high-dollar donor behavior, I suggest you consult several of the books listed below. Start with *Rocking the Ages*, which details extensive research findings that distinguish the formative experiences and values of the American public, generation by generation. Pay special attention to the Boomer generation, born 1946 through 1964, as they account for a large and fast-growing majority of the high-dollar market I'm writing about.

Then read *Ageless Marketing*. David Wolfe specializes in marketing to older Americans. His book is crammed with insight. So is Paul H. Ray and Sherry Ruth Anderson's *The Cultural Creatives*, which deals with much this same, ever-growing slice of the American population.

Axelrod, Terry B.: *Raising More Money: A Step by Step Guide to Building Lifelong Donors* (Boylston Books, 2000)

Burk, Penelope: *Donor-Centered Fundraising* (Burk & Associates, 2003)

Burnett, Ken: *Relationship Fundraising: A Donor Based Approach to the Business of Raising Money, 2nd Edition* (Jossey-Bass Publishers, 2002)

Ray, Paul H., and Sherry Ruth Anderson: *The Cultural Creatives: How 50 Million People Are Changing the World* (Three Rivers Press, 2001)

Smith, J. Walker, and Ann S. Clurman: *Rocking the Ages: The Yankelovich Report on Generational Marketing* (HarperBusiness, 1998)

Twist, Lynne: *The Soul of Money: Transforming Your Relationship with Money and Life* (W.W. Norton & Company, 2003)

Warwick, Mal: *How to Write Successful Fundraising Letters, Revised and Updated* (Jossey-Bass Publishers, 2001)

——: *Revolution in the Mailbox: Your Guide to Successful Direct Mail Fundraising* (Jossey-Bass Publishers, 2004)

Wolfe/103-1638884-5011005" Wolfe, David B., with Robert Snyder: *Ageless Marketing: Strategies for Reaching the Hearts and Minds of the New Customer Majority* (Dearborn Trade, a Kaplan Professional Company, 2003)

INDEX

Also by Emerson & Church, Publishers

Open Immediately: Straight Talk on Direct Mail Fundraising
Steven Hitchcock • 254 pp., $24.95 • ISBN 1889102121

If you want straight talk about direct mail fundraising, do what the title says: open this book immediately. In it you'll find 81 brief chapters examining every topic of importance to those who raise money by mail.

Unlike other books that over-complicate the subject, *Open Immediately!*, by Stephen Hitchcock, does just the opposite. It offers an elegantly simple — and inviting — approach to direct mail by focusing on one element at a time.

The book is divided into six major parts:
• Essentials of Direct Mail Fundraising
• Acquiring and Renewing Donors
• Targeting Your Mailings
• Writing Effective Letters
• Key Components of Your Appeal, and,
• How to Ask

Within each part, Hitchcock offers specific suggestions with just enough detail to allow you to implement his advice. Take the section, 'How to Ask.' Among the topics discussed are:
• Ways of asking for the gift
• Why it's important to ask for the gift at least twice
• When not to ask for a specific gift
• How to increase the very first gift (the one that dictates the size of further gifts),
• How to raise $1,000 gifts by mail, and
• How to ask for monthly gifts and charitable bequests
And that's just a sampling of the chapters.

Or take the section, 'Key Components of Your Appeal.' The 16 topics Hitchcock explores in these pages include a discussion of obsolete (and offensive) techniques, the cardinal rules of envelope copy, the misunderstood role of inserts, the use of multiple signatures, how to contain your costs, even a look at URGENT telegrams and whether they work.

Hitchcock knows you're not going to overturn your current program. But what you can do, he realizes, is tweak your efforts to be more profitable. And, *Open Immediately!* offers you dozens and dozens of ways to do just this.

The Relentlessly Practical Guide to Raising Serious Money
David Lansdowne • 240 pp., $24.95 • ISBN 1889102148

Why of all the hundreds of fund raising books available did AmeriCorps Vista, with offices throughout the U.S., single out *The Relentlessly Practical Guide to Raising Serious Money* as the premier book on the subject and provide a copy to thousands of its staff?

Why do a host of colleges and universities across the nation make Relentless an integral part of their fundraising courses?

Why do even fundraising consultants themselves refer to the book time and time again? Read David Lansdowne's acclaimed work and you'll quickly understand why.

No other writer in the field is as succinct, yet comprehensive. Nor do others have Lansdowne's trademark gift of extracting the essence of a technique and illuminating it in

Also by Emerson & Church, Publishers

unfailingly clear prose.

Lansdowne plumbs every major aspect of fundraising: from annual campaigns to capital campaigns, from major gifts to Internet fundraising, from planned giving to direct mail to prospect research.

Each chapter is delivered with heat-seeking precision. For example, do you want to know how to establish a gift club for donors? Turn to that chapter and chances are you'll learn more in the nine pages than you would from reading an entire book on the subject.

The same goes for attracting corporate support. Yes, you could spend hours boning up on the topic. But there's no need, as Lansdowne discusses everything you should know in a mere 11 pages.

There are other standout chapters that lift this book above others.

"The 16 Best Pieces of Fundraising Advice" may be the best rendering of its kind put to pen. "Fundraising's 20 Biggest Mistakes" is a masterful discussion alerting you to each and every red flag. "Fundraising Myths" explores more than a dozen pernicious myths that many are still bedevilled by. And, "What Every Board Member Must Know to Succeed," should be required reading for any trustee serving a gift-supported organization.

Here's 'real world' guidance you can put into practice literally today.

How to Write Knockout Proposals:
What You Must Know (and Say) to Win Funding Every Time
Joseph Barbato • 128 pp., $24.95 • ISBN 1889102202

If you've ever wondered why you were denied funding for an obviously worthy project, *How to Write Knockout Proposals* just may have the answer.

In all likelihood, your *proposal* – not your idea – was the problem.

Information abounds today – both online and in print -- and virtually anyone can identify the right prospects, whether they're corporations, foundations, or individuals. That's the easy part.

But few people, as Joseph Barbato says in the first chapter of his new book, can write a 'Knockout' proposal, "a document of such force it nearly catapults the funder down the hall."

A proposal writer himself for 30 years, Barbato hopes to change that.

Even if you don't have the skills to compose a *riveting* proposal – in other words, even if you're not Philip Roth, Joyce Carol Oates, or John Updike - you can still improve your proposal dramatically and distinguish it from the multitude of those being submitted today.

The key is to heed Barbato's tips and suggestions on everything from naming your proposal, to slanting its focus, to highlighting its compelling benefits, to identifying the best story to tell, to guarding against a series of red flags. And much more.

Barbato's engaging style goes down like icewater in August. He's brief, snappy, and always fresh. The entire book, with its 51 two-page chapters, can be read in one sitting. But don't be fooled by its brevity.

As Joel Orosz, the Kellogg Foundation's former program director, says in the Foreword: "As someone who has sat on both sides of the funding desk, I can attest that *How to Write Knockout Proposals* provides advice that will help you in the real world, with real funders."